Burnard's Self-Portrait (from the Dawes' Album).

A WAYWARD GENIUS

Neville Northy Burnard

CORNISH SCULPTOR

1818 - 1878

A WAYWARD GENIUS

Neville Northy Burnard

CORNISH SCULPTOR
1818 - 1878

A STUDY

by

MARY MARTIN

LODENEK PRESS

PADSTOW
CORNWALL

First published 1978

ISBN 0 902899 72 4 Hard Covers.
ISBN 0 902899 73 4 Paperback.

Printed in Great Britain by St. George Printing Works Ltd., Camborne.

TO IVY MAKER,
MY FIRST TEACHER

ACKNOWLEDGEMENTS

The author and publishers gratefully acknowledge the help of the following in compiling this book :

Mrs. Lawrence Maker of Callington, for access to her late husband's material on Burnard ; Mr. Trewin Copplestone of Bourton Grange, Berkshire, for access to the Dawes' album ; Rev. Brown, Rector of Camborne parish church ; Rev. Young, Rector of Altarnun ; Mr. H. L. Douch, curator of the Museum of the Royal Institution of Cornwall, Truro ; The Royal Cornwall Polytechnic Society, Falmouth ; Rev. D. A. Woods of Fowey ; the Trustees of Wesley Church, Camborne ; Mrs. Ann Treffry and Mrs. Blair of Place House, Fowey ; Mr. F. E. Lease; Mr. Otto Stanton; Rev. Barrie, Vicar of Bodmin; The Geological Museum, London ; Weston Park Museum, Sheffield ; the Trustees of Wesley Cottage, Trewint ; the Trustees of Launceston Museum ; Lady Sayer of Widecombe ; Mrs. Grace Kittow of Bude ; Mrs. A. C. Bizley of Perranporth ; Mr. P. W. Birkbeck ; Mr. F. J. Herring ; and many others.

For photographs we have been indebted to Jack Ingrey, and Derek Holmes of St. Merryn, Ray Bishop of Mulberry Studios, Wadebridge, David Hills of Camborne, Messrs. Bowling & Beauchamp of Sheffield, Roger Holmes of Liskeard, Ron Cable of Launceston, George Barnes of Padstow, H. Green of Weymouth and the Woolf-Greenham Collection, Newquay.

Our thanks are due to Messrs. Macmillan for permission to include Charles Causley's poem ' A Short Life of Neville Northy Burnard '.

CONTENTS

LIST OF ILLUSTRATIONS

35 Bust of Joseph Thomas Treffry, in Place House, executed by Burnard at the height of his powers.

36 Tombstone to James Whitburn (Gwennap Church), carved by Burnard, aged 15.

37 Marble bust of the Prince of Wales (later Edward VII): a royal commission for Burnard (in Polytechnic Hall, Falmouth).

38 Medallion portrait of Mrs. Catherine Enys (in Truro Museum).

39 Marble bust of Richard Trevithick (in Truro Museum).

40-42 Statue of Richard Lander, upper Lemon Street, Truro : erected in 1852.

43 Bust of Richard Lander, reputedly by Burnard.

44 Dr. William Borlase: plaster bust (in Truro Museum).

45 Portrait of an unknown gentleman, by Burnard (pencil: in Truro Museum).

46 Portrait of Rev. William Rowe, Vicar of St. Teath (pencil: in Truro Museum).

47 Burnard's memorial to Dr. George Smith, in Wesley Church, Camborne.

48-49 Statue of Ebenezer Elliott, the 'Corn Law Rhymer'; 1854 (in Weston Park, Sheffield).

50 Bronze bust of John Couch Adams, astronomer, of Laneast.

51 'A great, powerful, pugilistic-looking fellow' — Burnard's self-portrait, about 1850.

52 Professor Edward Forbes: marble by Burnard (in Geological Museum, London).

53 G. B. Greenough, F.R.S., founder of the Geological Society (in Geological Museum, London): 1850.

54 Marble bust of William Makepeace Thackeray, the novelist, posthumously executed (about 1867). Copy now at National Portrait Gallery.

55 Medallion of Olive Louise Burnard, aged 2 ; executed by Burnard in 1875.

56 Memorial to Michael Williams, engineer (in Gwennap Church); reputedly by Burnard.

57 Harry Dawe.

58 Frederick Dawe.

59 Miss (? Bessy) Dawe.

60 Lizzie Jope, neé Dawe.

61 Maud Dawe.

62 Gertie Dawe.

63-64 Poems inscribed in the Dawes' Album.

65 Burnard's pencil drawing of the Cheesewring.

66 Trethevy Quoit (drawn for the Dawes' Album).

67 Pencil portrait of Samuel Drew, metaphysician, by Burnard (from Dawes' Album).

68 The face Burnard could not caricature (from the Dawes' Album).

69 Rev. Hugh Rogers: one of Burnard's finest marble sculptures (in Camborne Church).

70 Slate tombstone erected in memory of Burnard by Camborne Old Cornwall Society.

Appendix B : (p. 57) A Defence of the Church of England.

Appendix C : Memorial to Lottie Burnard and Tom Nicholson.

A SHORT LIFE OF
NEVILLE NORTHY BURNARD

Cornish sculptor 1818-1878

Here lived Burnard who with his finger's bone
Broke syllables of light from the moorstone,
Spat on the genesis of dust and clay,
Rubbed with huge hands the blinded eyes of day,
And through the seasons of the talking sun
Walked, calm as God, the fields of Altarnun.

Here, where St. Nonna with a holy reed
Hit the bare granite, made the waters bleed,
Madmen swam to their wits in her clear well.
Young Burnard fasted, watched, learned how to tell
Stone beads under the stream, and at its knock
Quietly lifted out his prize of rock.

As Michaelangelo by stone possessed
Sucked the green marble from his mother's breast
So Burnard, at his shoulder the earth's weight,
Received on his child's tongue wafers of slate
And when he heard his granite hour strike
Murdered Christ's hangman with a mason's spike.

The village sprawled white as a marriage bed,
Gulls from the north coast stumbled overhead
As Burnard, standing in the church-yard hay,
Leaned on the stiff light, hacked childhood away,
On the tomb slabs watched bugler, saint, dove,
Under his beating fists grow big with love.

The boy with the Laocoön's snake crown
Caught with a six-inch nail the stinking town.
He turned, as Midas, men to stone, then gold.
Forgot, he said, what it was to be cold.
Birds rang like coins. He spread his fingers wide.
Wider the gulfs of love as his child died.

Packing only his heart, a half-hewn stone,
He left house, clothes, goods, blundered off alone:
London to Cornwall and the spinning moor,
Slept in stacks, hedges, barns, retraced the spoor
Of innocence ; through the lost shallows walked,
Of his dead child, they say, for ever talked.

9

At last, the dragged November sun on high,
Burnard lay in a mumpers' inn to die.
At Redruth Workhouse, with the stripped, insane,
Banged on death's door and did not bang in vain ;
Rocked in a gig to sleep in paupers' clay
Where three more warmed his side till judgement day.

No mourner stood to tuck him in God's bed,
Only the coffin-pusher. Overhead,
The fishing rooks unravelling the hour,
Two men, a boy, restored Camborne Church tower.
' This box ', the clerk said, ' holds your man in place '.
' We come ', they said, ' to smooth dirt from his face '.

No cross marks the spot where he first saw day.
Time with a knife wears the dull flesh away,
Peels the soft skin of blocks cut on the green
Signed by a boy, ' *Burnard. Sculptor. Thirteen.*'
Slowly the land shakes as the ocean's gun
Sounds over Cornwall. He stares from the sun.

The torn tramp, rough with talents, walks the park.
Children have swift stones ready. Men, dogs, bark.
The light falls on the bay, the cold sea leaks,
The slate face flushes, opens its lips, speaks.
In from the moor the pointing shadows flock,
Finger, beneath the river, the pure rock.

Charles Causley

PREFACE

During my early years I often heard the name of Neville Northy Burnard mentioned in my home-area. He was a sculptor born near my locality in the village of Altarnun on Bodmin Moor, Cornwall, in 1818 ; he was the son of a humble stonemason ; he rose to become one of the foremost portrait sculptors in London, to whom it was thought fashionable to sit ; and he died a penniless vagrant in the paupers' hospital at Redruth, West Cornwall. Beyond these hard facts I knew little. I had seen a few early works of Burnard at Altarnun — in the churchyard there is a delicately cut slate-headstone executed by him as a fourteen-year-old boy, and a weathered stone head of John Wesley in the niche of the Georgian Wesleyan chapel just across the road from the church. Also I had noticed the highly-finished marble portrait of Mrs. Enys in Truro museum. Apart from these, I had no idea of the prolific variety in Burnard's output.

My interest was reawakened after hearing that there was a memorial service at Altarnun in 1968 commemorating the 150th anniversary of Burnard's birth. After reading Charles Causley's fine poem it seemed to me that a man who could inspire such powerful imagery, and whose life ended so tragically, deserved more attention than the scanty references I had previously read. I started to inquire into the circumstances of his career, and the more I saw of his work, the more fascinated I became at its inseparability from Burnard's Cornish environment.

Throughout his successful career in London, Burnard made frequent journeys back to Cornwall, both to visit friends and relations and to exhibit at the Royal Cornwall Polytechnic Society at Falmouth. He never tried to deny his rural breeding, and in fact, made a point of hunting out commissions connected with his native land. His letters are full of his concern at leaving statuesque records of Cornish men and women of letters, science and public esteem. The pains Burnard took to keep faith with his country origins found their ultimate, most poignant expression, in the last years of his life. He closed up his once thriving London studio and returned to Cornwall for good. For three years he tramped over the countryside which once had been the scene of his youthful aspirations. Aimlessly passing from one household to the next, exchanging sketches, poems and verbal entertainment for his hospitality, he last visited Altarnun in 1877. Here he stayed for a few weeks with just a bundle of clothes, boarding with his schoolfriend Samuel Pearn, and sleeping in the nearby lodging house at Five Lanes. His searchings and drunken wandering were eventually terminated by death from a heart and kidney complaint in Redruth Workhouse.

I would suggest that to his early years and apprenticeship we may attribute Burnard's broad, varied approach to sculpture. As an ambitious, knowledge-seeking young lad, responsive to all aspects of art and nature, his potentiality as an original sculptor was greatest in the initial stage of his career. It is true that his later connections with the mainstreams of British and Continental art were extremely valuable to him, and that the knowledge he gained from direct contact with leading artists, scientists, philosophers and politicians all contributed to his education (which previously had been self-taught and laborious). However, Burnard's later sculpting technique, at the so-called peak of his career, became stereotyped into the popular style so acceptable to nineteenth-century society. Although masterly and finely-wrought and much sought-after, his portrait works at this time often appear a little sterile and habitual. They seem too often to lack the individualism, the enthusiastic experimentation and variety of the younger artist.

I have therefore concentrated on the Cornish aspect of Burnard's career: on his early influences, the works he prepared in Cornwall (and which I regard as inextricably linked to the Cornish scene) ; and the variety of architectural and sculptural styles, the traditional slate and stone masonry which was his heritage.

There was also a practical reason for choosing Burnard's Cornish connections. Looking into his London career — spanning some thirty years — I was unable to come upon much information. In the London libraries, galleries and collections I could only find lists of works (mainly commissioned marble portraits), their dates and entries into the Royal Academy exhibitions. With the exception of the Geological Museum, which houses two busts by him, I have been unsuccessful in tracing these works. I can only assume that many have been lost. (For facts relating to Burnard's output, see Appendices D and E.)

Research in Cornwall however, was more rewarding. Many local libraries had preserved old newspapers and periodicals, which yielded up proud contemporary reports on Burnard's progress as a humble Cornish lad entering through the portals of fame and prosperity the London artistic and social scene. I visited Burnard's home area on Bodmin Moor, and talked to old folk who recall their relatives' accounts of meetings with him. Families still tended to stay in the same village, so there was no problem of breakdown in communication. Information was not lost, though it might often be distorted by time and the spoken word. Memories are long in country districts, and often one person has been able to recommend me to another who has a piece of work or a story about Burnard.

This all led me to a more direct appreciation of Burnard's character, production and background. Finally, by coming upon and studying the artist's work at leisure in the local churches, graveyards, museums and homes, the man himself became alive for me. By coming into contact with that countryside, architecture and pattern of life, which has, as in his own time, remained largely rural and sparsely populated, it was possible to recapture something of the atmosphere which nurtured the sculptor's attitudes and his growth as both man and artist.   M.M.

ONE

EARLY YEARS IN ALTARNUN

Reader! Have you yet been at Altarnun?
The best and largest parish in the county.
(Take some of this in earnest, some in fun)
The greatest sharer in Dame Nature's bounty —
If rocks and bogs, and commons, wild and wide
As Nature's *bounties* may be specified.

Its small metropolis is named Penpont
And is or might be made a pleasant place.
I've lately been informed (but then, I don't
Believe it) — that it now improves apace ;
Well! nowhere 'twixt the candle and the tomb,
Will any place more give improvement *room*.

It held a vicarage, a church and school ;
A mill, some cots, 2 taverns and a shop,
One domine, one parson, and one fool,
(A *natural*) and some who 'liked a drop'.
Among the worst of whom was Farmer Venning
A sample of whose daily life I'm penning.

I had forgot to mention that a chapel,
Sacred to good John Wesley, too was there,
Where some for pastime went, and some to grapple
With fears and doubts in strong and earnest prayer,
Though I should deem the *closet* fitted best
For humble suppliants for peace and rest.

(*From* 'A Village Hampden', *written by Burnard in the Dawes' album.*)

Neville Northy Burnard was born on October 11, 1818 at Penpont, Altarnun, in a cottage typical of the Bodmin Moor area with its mullioned windows and newel staircase. Altarnun is Cornwall's largest and most scantily populated parish. Burnard's father, George, was a stonemason and his mother, Jane, ran a dame-school (making straw bonnets in her spare time) where Neville was taught the rudimentary three R's. He left school, as was usual, at ten years old, to act as mortar-boy to his father. This involved handing to and fro plaster, brick and stone in all weathers on laborious building jobs, often in spots isolated in the heart of the moor. But his mind soon travelled to higher things and, much to his father's disparagement, often applied himself to drawing and to carving angels, men, flora and fauna on an old oak door. Neville eventually turned his hand to slate-incising, improvising chisels by grinding six-inch nails.

The Parish

Altarnun still stands relatively isolated from the main thoroughfare. It can be reached by the road which leaves Bodmin Moor for Launceston. It comprises a narrow, winding village street with cottages running downhill to Penpont Water, a moorland stream crossed by a hump-backed bridge leading to the fifteenth century church of St. Nonna. The tower of 109 feet is one of the highest in Cornwall; the church is often referred to as the 'Cathedral of the Moor', for its beauty and majestic serenity.

It was only in 1769 that a turnpike road replaced the medieval tracks serving Altarnun. This enabled mail coaches from Penzance to London to bypass Altarnun. The 1811 Survey of the Parish states that in Penpont (the village over the bridge from the Church) there were ten families: three in agriculture, five in trades, manufacture or handicrafts, and two in other work. There were twenty-two males and twenty-four females.

For centuries the inhabitants of Altarnun were small moorland farmers, tin-streamers and artisans. In fact, the Burnard family comprised a large proportion of the latter class. The two families of longest standing in the parish were those of Burnard and Isbell; both were stoneworkers and both were represented on the 1641 Protestation Roll, and the 1671 Church Rate. As a sculptor, Neville had a long tradition of inherited skills behind him. Just a few of his relatives were James Isbell (1756-1840), who built Dartmoor prison, and Robert Whale, A.R.A. (1805-87), of Burnard descent. Members of the Isbell family were two sculptors, Robert of Stonehouse (1769-1824) and his son, James of Truro (1787-1837). Their work is to be seen in many churches in Devon and Cornwall.

Methodism and the Wesleys

The two families of Burnard and Isbell intermarried in 1739 with the wedding of Elizabeth (1717-1805), Neville's aunt and daughter of Thomas and Catherine Burnard, to Digory Isbell (c.1718-95).

Burnard was thus part of the close-knit community of Altarnun. He was also part of that society which had come to welcome John Wesley and Methodism as its way of life. Neville's connections with Wesleyanism must have been strengthened on his hearing again and again those stories passed down through his aunt Elizabeth. She and her husband Digory were among the first to receive Wesley's followers, then so unpopular, and bring their neighbours to hear them preach. Later the couple built on to the little cottage at Trewint a ' prophets' chamber ' for their guests. One room for preaching in, one for sleeping in, just like the Shunamite woman made for Elisha's use — the Bible passage which Elizabeth read and followed as her guide-line.

Wesley himself was struck by the fervour of the Altarnun people and the growing success of Methodism. On his fourth visit to Trewint in 1745, he remarked: "Indeed I never remember so great an awakening in Cornwall, wrought in so short a time, among young and old, rich and poor, from Trewint quite to the sea-side ".

In the tiny prophets' chamber at Trewint, now preserved as a museum, there is a most delicately carved shell-cameo of the hymn-writer James Montgomery. It was carved by Burnard, reputedly with a penknife at the age of twelve. (See Illustration 6.)

In 1795 the early Methodist society transferred its meeting place from the Isbells' home to a chapel at Altarnun churchtown. In 1836, when this chapel next door to Burnard's birthplace was enlarged, Neville sculpted a head of Wesley in polyphant stone. He was then eighteen. The sculpture was placed over the doorway where it may still be seen.

Many years later it became Burnard's custom to do a drawing of Wesley copied from a hymn-book portrait, and present it to any Methodist family who was giving him hospitality.

Burnard lived in a period when both scientific enquiry and Christian fortitude were prominent spirits. When he later visited the broad-minded Quaker home of the Foxes in Falmouth, he could not have failed to be impressed by the stimulating conversation, and the pursuit of knowledge by all the artists and scientists who frequented the house at Penjerrick. The Fox family in turn were impressed by Burnard's simple bearing, by his candid nature and unaffected approach to sculpture.

Methodism, in Burnard's day, had not resolved itself into that stern, High-Victorian, guilt-ridden type of moral outlook, which it took on in later years, and which is often found in Cornwall. At the end of the eighteenth century (Wesley died in 1791) Cornish Methodists had remained, according to Wesley's wishes, united with the Church. Remarkably, this attitude continued in Altarnun until 1934. In the churchyard the Isbells are buried near Burnard's grandfather. Their inscription was, during Neville's boyhood, a source of pride in the family. (Perhaps it gave rise to the legend he must have been raised on: If one runs round the Isbell tomb

15

twelve times and puts one's fingers in one's ears, the bells of Heaven can be heard!) The inscription on the altar-tomb includes the following:

'They were the first who entertained the Methodist preachers in this county and lived and died in that connection, but strictly adhered to the Duties of the Established Church. Reader, may thy end be like theirs'.

Throughout his career Burnard sculpted prominent public figures of both the established Church and Methodist Connexion with impartial appreciation of their dedicated moral fibre. Such figures include Gerald Massey (poet and mystic), James Montgomery, Reverend Hugh Rogers, George Smith (Wesleyan missionary), and Father Gavazzi.

2 Plaque on Burnard's Birthplace, erected in 1968.

3 The former Wesley Chapel, adjoining Burnard's birthplace.

4 Head of John Wesley, sculpted by Burnard, on the Chapel.

5 Wesley Cottage, Trewint, home of Digory and Elizabeth Isbell, Burnard's relatives.

6 Shell cameo of James Montgomery, by
Burnard aged 12 (in Wesley Cottage,
Trewint).

7 Tombstone to Grace Burnard, carved
by Burnard at age 12 (now in Truro
Museum).

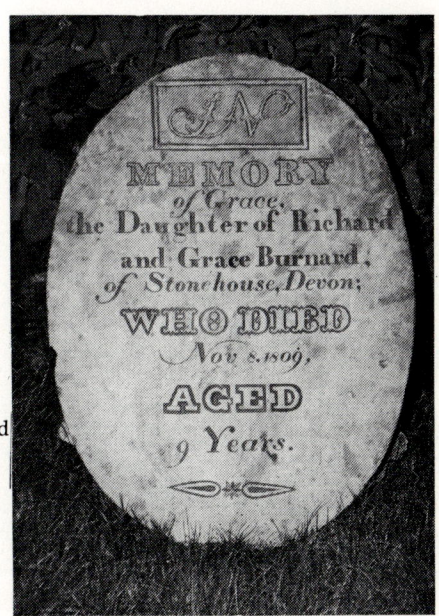

8   Detail of tombstone in Altarnun Churchyard, carved at age 13.

9   Tombstone to Burnard's grandparents,
carved at age 14.

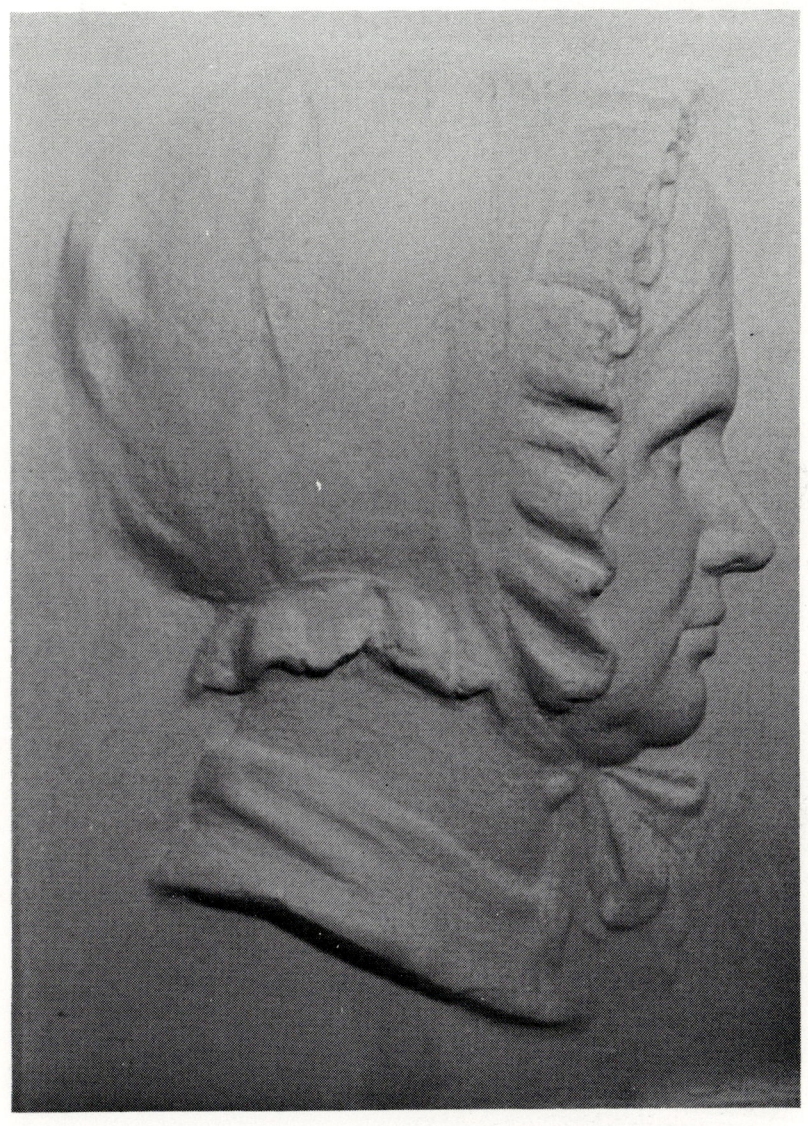

10   Burnard's mother (medallion in Truro Museum).

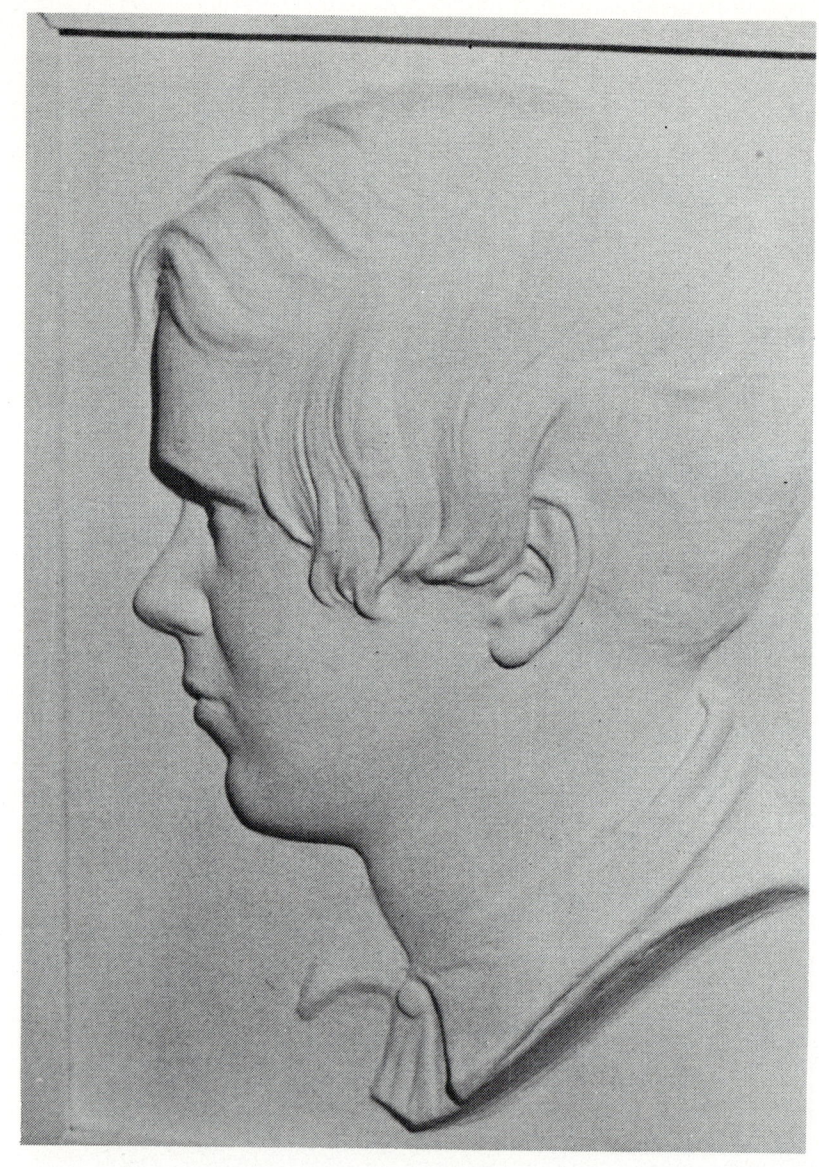

11   Self-portrait by Burnard, aged about 14 (in Truro Museum).

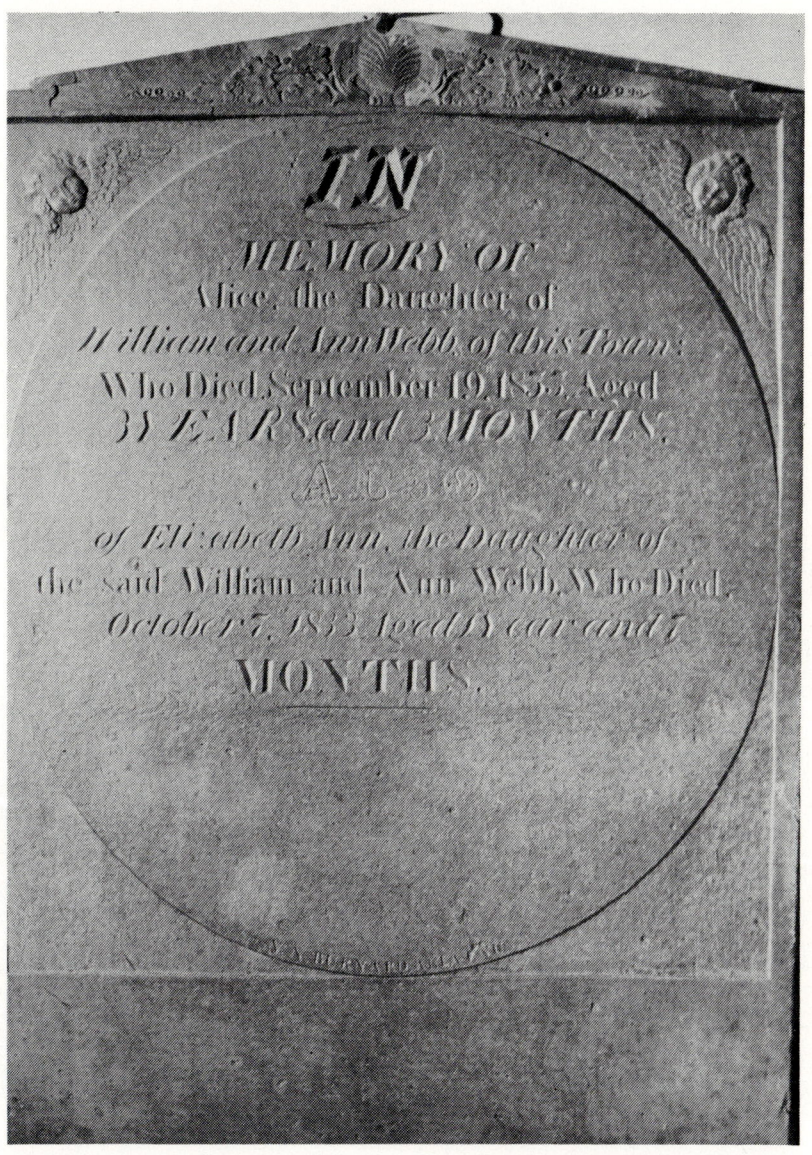

12   The Webb Memorial (1833) in Bodmin Church.

13 Detail of the Cundy tomb,
Lewannick ; by Towl, ' schoolmaster and
engraver.'

14 Details of tombstone by Burnard's
father, in Altarnun Churchyard.

16 Mary Magdalene : medieval sculpture on east wall of St. Mary's Church, Launceston.

17 Medieval bench end, Altarnun.

18 Grotesque figure, sculpted in slate by the young Burnard
(in Truro Museum).

19-24 Examples of the rich heritage of 15th century bench ends in Altarnun Church.

19-24 Examples of the rich heritage of 15th century bench ends in Altarnun Church.

19-24 Examples of the rich heritage of 15th century bench ends in Altarnun Church.

14TH CENTURY OCTAGONAL FONT
ST·BARTHOLOMEW'S CHURCH - LOSTWITHIEL.

NORMAN FONT OF CATACLEUSE
STONE AT ST·NICHOLAS - FOWEY
FIMBRARUS

25 Three Cornish fonts.

NORMAN FONT -
ALTARNUN

26 Head of Homer, carved for the
Exhibition of the Polytechnic Society,
Falmouth : executed by Burnard at age 13.

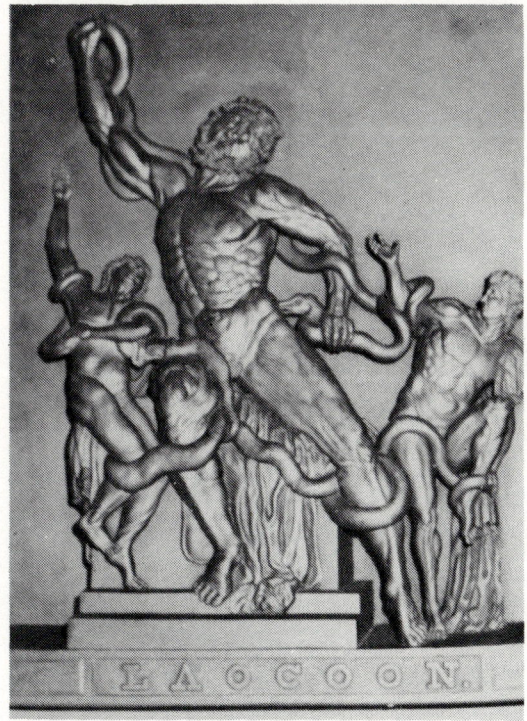

27 The Laocoön, executed at age 16
(in Polytechnic Hall, Falmouth).

28   The 17th century Spoure Memorial, in North Hill Church ; one of
Cornwall's finest monuments.

30 Tombstone to Arthur Peter, by
Burnard ; in North Hill Churchyard.

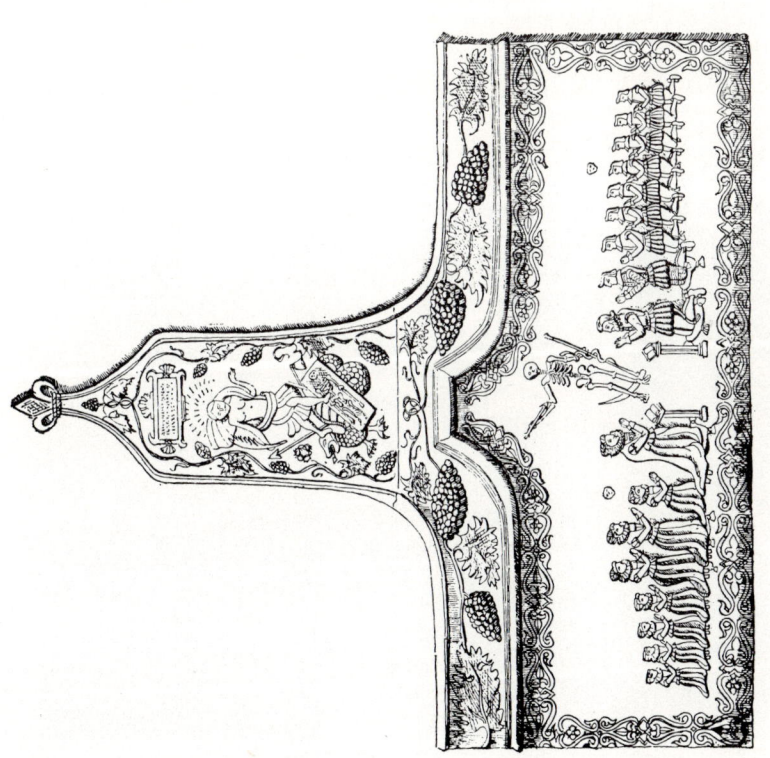

29 The Vincent family slate memorial
in North Hill Church (drawn by
Alice C. Bizley).

31 The Rashleigh Arms ; one of the
shields carved by Burnard for the
National School, Tywardreath.

32 The late 16th century Rashleigh
family memorial in Fowey Church : an
inspiration to the young sculptor ?

TWO

TRADITIONAL BUILDING MATERIALS IN CORNWALL

Granite

Cornwall's buildings are predominantly of granite and slate; the countryside does not provide rich supplies of timber for building. Granite, with its coarse grain, is not adaptable for small detail, and traditional carvers have tended to express their feeling for decoration in a broad, unified handling. Bodmin Moor, which surrounds Altarnun, is one of the four main granite-producing areas — the other three being the Hensbarrow region, near St. Austell, the Downs between Falmouth, Camborne and Helston, and the whole of Penwith, the Land's End peninsula.

Prior to the seventeenth century, unquarried granite or 'moorstone' blocks found lying were used for wall and house-building materials. Before the end of the Middle Ages, masons were experienced in dressing the stone suitably for church building. Huge boulders can still be seen in use as clapper bridges, horse and cattle troughs, and let into walls, gateposts and stiles. The medieval masons were so adept at fitting the odd-shaped stones that many buildings have stood the centuries without mortar. In Altarnun Church each base, pier and capital making up the whole pillar is one piece of moorstone worked over by hand.

The only alternative local stones which could be used for sculpting and decorating were elvan, red porphyry (a pedestal of which once supported Burnard's bust of the Prince of Wales), Cataclewse stone (as in the font at Fowey church), serpentine from the Lizard area, and Polyphant. This last stone, quarried a mile or so from Altarnun, contains silicates of magnesium and iron which give it a sombre grey-blue appearance, often spotted with reds and browns. This was the stone Burnard used for his Wesley portrait.

Slate

The material with which Burnard seemed wholly at ease in his early years was slate. One can immediately see in the intuitive feel for the qualities of the material, and in the patient finish of his early tombstones, the rare perfectionism which he was to achieve in the marble works of his maturity.

In Burnard's day the great slate quarry at Delabole (near Cornwall's North coast) was yielding vast amounts of slate to be used for many purposes; and there were still plenty of craftsmen skilled in its quarrying, preparation and carving. This stone can often be seen in moorland walls, water-tanks, roofs and tombstones. Local slate was so plentiful that from the eighteenth century it became customary to hang walls with it. Many houses and shop-fronts are slate-hung in the market-towns of Liskeard and Launceston, close to

Altarnun. Delabole slate is renowned for its endurance. It is finely-grained, quick-drying, non-porous, impervious to frost and relatively light.

The peak of expertise in slate-cutting in Cornwall seems to have been around 1570-1650. The use of slate goes back more than four centuries. It is a metamorphic stone, quarried from the Devonian rocks. Its appearance in building, both monumental and everyday, is so frequent it is often referred to as 'Cornish marble'. The gentry and merchants of Elizabeth's Cornwall found it an ideal material for their monuments. As its cost was moderate, yeoman families were also enabled to employ it.

Slate tombs and reliefs are fairly common in Cornish churches. It is evident that Burnard saw and noted the motifs and competent techniques which occur repeatedly in them. Many early monuments feature boldly carved figures of men and women, standing in high relief. Numerous marble portraits by Burnard were executed in this manner. Alice Bizley in her book *The Slate Figures of Cornwall* has recorded that 64 slate portraits still exist in 47 of Cornwall's parish churches, and that the majority of carved figures are in the north and east; i.e. in Burnard's locality. The earliest figured slate is 1500, the latest 1727 — the memorial to Sarah Cottel at Kilkhampton.

In North Hill church is such a slate, of which Burnard would have been aware when a small boy. (At the age of fifteen he in fact engraved a slate tombstone to Arthur Peter in the churchyard there.) The tomb inside is to Thomas Vincent of Batten and his wife Jane, 1606. It is a remarkable piece of work: an elaborate altar-tomb with the eight sons and seven daughters well-modelled. On the front and back panels is an allegorical representation of the Ascension of Christ, and below a figure of death. It is probably the work of the master sculptor who also carved similar slabs in the vicinity: the Mannington tomb at Stoke Climsland in 1605, the Trefusis at Lezant in 1606, and Durant at Bodmin, 1608.

Later carvers worked in low relief, and eventually in the more familiar incised line with which they achieved more detail and lessened flaking. This last treatment was handed down well into Burnard's day. He, however, often reverted to the older, low-relief method in his lettering, and made an impression by raising the letters, carving them in relief so that they would withstand the weather. Even in his later marbles (like those of Hugh Rogers and George Smith) Burnard seems to hark back to the high-relief slates he saw as a boy; his medallion-type portraits rise from the background from which they are moulded.

The best materials and sculptors were employed by the more important families; the lesser gentry and yeoman made do with slate from the nearest quarries, carved by local masons. However, this meant that many tombs cut locally were individual in style: although the proportions of the human body were often beyond the grasp of local artisans, the drawing on these slates shows solid and attractive lettering, and an independence of the stylized patterns of professional carvers.

In the sixteenth and seventeenth centuries, pattern books and Books of Emblems were issued by the Low Countries book-sellers. Despite this, the humbler eighteenth century local churchyard carvings seem often to have escaped the general trend to 'improve' upon clumsy designs and awkward composition. The late eighteenth century stones in Lewannick and Altarnun churchyards display a naïve and vivacious sensitivity. The Cundy tombstone at Lewannick is by Towl, schoolmaster and engraver. The first letter from the inscription exemplifies the delicacy of late eighteenth-century writing, and the refinement to which local modest carvers aspired.

The two medallions (illustration 14) are from a slate carved by Burnard's father, and seem to be established motifs fairly common in other churchyards. There are identical patterns on a tomb in Linkinhorne, carved by Daniel Gumb (born 1703 ; a stonemason, hermit and astronomer who lived in a cave below the Cheeswring, on Caradon Moor). Frequently from the eighteenth century one encounters crudely-sketched death's-heads and wings of angels. Burnard often took these and refined them down into more sculptural faces.

Burnard's Early Work with Slate

In Burnard's day there was no machinery for facing slate slabs. After trimming them into shape it was essential to render the surface as smooth as a plate by continuous rubbing with a French millstone, water and fine sand fetched from Dozmary pool six miles away.

At twelve Burnard surprised his father by cutting a small head-stone for his nine-year-old cousin's grave. The letters were carved out into relief with long sharpened nails. At fourteen he prepared a tombstone to his grandparents — 'Sacred to the memory of George and Elizabeth Burnard'. At the head of the inscription is a fine relief of an eagle in flight against the sun's rays, with embellishments of delicate weeping-willow fronds and a regularly-patterned raised first word.

In North Hill the fifteen year-old Burnard adapted in his own way the willow motif which was often used by local contemporary engravers — Wadge, William Parry and Wannick. If one compares Burnard's tomb to Peter with Wadge's more clumsy willow on the grave to James Coombe (1878), it is easy to see Burnard's flexibility and lighter touch. In Bodmin Church is a stone by the fifteen-year-old Burnard to William and Ann Webb. At the top it bears a scallop shell, two cherubs and vine branches, and clearly demonstrates Burnard's love for slate and his feeling for its material qualities.

When he was thirteen Burnard modelled a bas-relief (9 by 6 inches) of Homer and incised a delicate decorative border, polishing the surface until it shone like silver. It is now in the library of the Royal Polytechnic Society at Falmouth, together with his small bas-relief of the Laocoön. This precocious work (executed at sixteen) Burnard based on a woodcut from the Penny Magazine, creating a marvellously animated effect. The finished surface gleams like silver, and so sure was he of his deftness that he was able to cut out the head of Laocoön and replace it with barely a join-line apparent. It was entered into the first Polytechnic Society's exhibition (newly formed by Anna Maria and Caroline Fox of Penjerrick). Widely acclaimed, the relief was awarded a first Silver Medal.

In 1836 Burnard's entry was 'Christ Bearing the Cross', for which he received a Bronze Medal. In 1837 he was again given a Bronze for his 'Jupiter and Thetis.' And it was a piece of slate-carving that gained Burnard his entry into the higher realms of sculpture. Sir Charles Lemon, M.P., of Carclew and first President of the Polytechnic Society, was convinced that Burnard would benefit from the more fertile atmosphere in London. To this end Lemon introduced him to Sir Francis Chantrey, London's most famous sculptor at that time. As a test-piece Burnard chose to sculpt, with his own homemade chisels, a piece of slate. Upon it he adroitly fashioned a realistic farmyard scene of a sow and her farrow. Chantrey was suitably impressed.

It is now generally appreciated that Burnard's proficiency and artistry in slate-carving was the result of a rare touch, and an inbred love for the stone of his native land. In 1954, Camborne Old Cornwall Society erected a simple, inscribed piece of Delabole slate on Burnard's previously unmarked grave. In 1968 Charles Causley designed a circular slate tablet for the wall of Burnard's birthplace; this was drawn up by Joseph Setchell, executed by a St. Breward craftsman at the Delabole quarry, and was unveiled during the 150th anniversary of Burnard's birth in 1968.

THREE

BACKGROUND, EARLY EMPLOYMENT AND COMMISSIONS
1833-52

When Burnard won the Silver Medal for his slate relief of the Laocoön, the Royal Cornwall Polytechnic Society's Report of 1835 referred to him as:

> 'A youth of 16 who had executed in an obscure village without instruction and with rude tools of his own making a carving in relief of the Laocoön, in Delabole slate, his only pattern being a woodcut of the well-known figures on a frontispiece of the Penny Magazine."

However, one should beware of the widespread belief that Neville Burnard was living in a cultural desert, starved of stimulating aesthetic influences. It is plain that his feeling for form and life, his basic sense of design and unity demonstrated in his Laocoön, were derived from sources additional to a 'woodcut from the Penny Magazine.' An impressionable, open and sensitive character like Burnard could, through an honest approach, learn much from merely observing and studying nature and the buildings and growth around him.

When Joseph Treffry of Place House, Fowey, sent up for the leading masons of south-east Cornwall to undertake extensions and alterations to his property, he was calling upon some of the most skilled sculptors in the country — craftsmen who had behind them generations of inherited aptitude in stone and wood-working. The labours of all those painters and decorators engaged at Fowey were mainly organized by John Whale, a discerning tradesman from Altarnun. Whale took the fifteen year-old Neville down to Place, where he was employed at stone-carving and modelling in plaster numerous medallions and embellishments.

Burnard's high artistic standards can be comprehended if one realizes the early influence exerted upon him of Altarnun church. Stylistically the church incorporates within its architecture the best flowerings of the Norman, Medieval and Renaissance ages. All these universal styles are common all over Europe, but here they seem cast into a particular localized mould, characteristic of the Bodmin Moor area.

Altarnun Church

Since Celtic times the huge moorland parish of Altarnun had been a central Christian meeting place. Of the sixth century church of St. Nonna (the mother of St. David of Wales), nothing remains except the Cornish Cross at the gate, and the Holy Well renowned for curing madness. The font is the only thing left from the second church that the Normans built. Heavy and statuesque, is bears four bearded heads at each corner, with large rosettes in between. Like so many other Cornish fonts, this granite composition shows a rare wholeness and individual workmanship, of which Burnard cannot have been ignorant.

In the fifteenth century the present church was begun. It is an outstanding building of moorstone which, with its tall pinnacled tower, took over a generation to complete. The aisles retain their marvellously carved waggon roofs and bosses ; both north and south porches also have original carved barrel roofs. The two aisles have broad four-light Perpendicular windows, of a design which brings two lights together under one pointed arch: a feature particularly popular in the district. A fifteenth-century rood screen ran across the nave and aisles, each section with two lights having Perpendiculai tracery and two panels of blank tracery at the base. The altar rails were made in 1684 by John Gard, a carpenter from Launceston. The baluster shapes indicate the Jacobean style.

However, it is the extraordinary collection of carved bench-ends which attracts and holds one's attention on entering the church. Burnard, it seems, drew upon the design and technique displayed in these bench-ends many times. There are seventy-nine remaining bench-ends, all carved between 1510 and 1530 (the time it took the Altarnun people to raise the money for both seats and bench-ends). An angel on one of the ends bears an inscription: 'Robert Daye, Maker of this Work'.

It is in these richly chiselled oak panels that we can see something of the history of the decorative style which was peculiar to Cornwall. In these, as in other Cornish bench-ends, there is a riot of ornament which seems to present that reaction against the less flamboyant Perpendicular style of 1400 to 1460. After 1460 Cornwall seems to have reverted to a more exaggerated decoration, a taste which appears to have originated in her Celtic past — those abundant scrolls and convoluted forms in granite crosses, stones, manuscripts and beam carvings. This sense of embellishment lasted well into the Renaissance period. In Burnard's home locality it expressed itself in the detailed exteriors of the churches at Bodmin, St. Neot and Launceston. At Altarnun the bench-ends can be divided into three categories. The Reverend W. A. Kneebone saw them as *Religious subjects* (for example, of angels holding symbols of the Crucifixion, and St. George in contemporary dress — slashed sleeves and breeches and the doublet of a courtier); *Parish Worthies and Common Sights* (a wealth of humanity — particular portraits, a diabolic-looking jester, men playing bagpipes and the fiddle, and sheep grazing on the hill-sides); and *Renaissance Designs* — (those decorative motifs common to most European religious sculpturing — scrolls, curvilinear shapes and paired grotesques).

In Truro museum is a slate carving by the young Burnard some one foot square. It is a caricatured profile of a man with a beard, medieval hat and hood, and is presented as a medallion set in a square. To give emphasis to the profile, the slate is skilfully cut through to the back. This youthful work bears an uncanny resemblance to a bench-end in Altarnun church: the panel near the belfry contains a carving which in subject-matter and treatment seems positively to have inspired Burnard's early design. The flat plane of the wood-panel has (as in the others), been pitted with small, regular circles made with a circular-type chisel. Burnard had obviously tried to simulate this effect in slate. He used the circular motif later on in his portrait reliefs as a means of livening up the flat background.

Launceston

There has always been a stylistic thread running through the churches of Launceston, Altarnun and Fowey (where Burnard was early employed). Influence between these three districts is apparent from the sixteenth to the nineteenth centuries; the same families of masons plied back and forth using their repeated skills and qualities of expression throughout the generations.

Launceston is about nine miles from Altarnun, situated on the eastern edge of Bodmin Moor. Until 1835 it was the Assize town for Cornwall as well as the region's main agricultural centre, which partly explains why its grand eighteenth-century houses could afford to be built of red brick, so scarce in Cornwall. Burnard must have visited Launceston regularly, with his father on his building jobs, and to attend the weekly markets which dealt with a large number of Bodmin Moor's livestock. The town is dominated by the precipitous Norman castle of Dunheved with its medieval south-gate set on an incline. Crooked slate-hung, granite-built houses and low, covered alleys merge with the lovely symmetrical Georgian houses and substantial square; the whole aspect is one of a varied but unified, compact arrangement. Most Cornish churches are plain and massively built to withstand the rough weather; but the exterior of St. Mary Magdalene church, standing in the middle of Launceston, presents a wealth of decoration. It epitomizes the Celtic sense of intricate decoration — contrasting with the more restrained style practised elsewhere at this time. Standing beneath the dark sober fourteenth-century elvan stone tower, this effect is all the more emphatically seen. The church was the gift of Sir Henry Trecarrel in memory of his son and wife. Between 1511 and 1524 he insisted upon employing those masons who were already engaged on working at the intricate exteriors of Place House, Fowey. The Launceston facade, all formed from moorland granite, probably excels Place in its teeming detail. There are quatrefoils, coats of arms, fleurs de lys; roses, thistles, pomegranates and palm-leaves, and a beautiful

recumbent Mary Magdalene surrounded by minstrels. It is quite
evident from this building that both Cornish craftsmen and the
granite they fashioned were capable of a high level of sculpture.
When left to develop and improvise their own styles, these masons
created a wealth of individual detail. They quite naturally combined
the secular with the religious, and presented the colloquial, the
earthy and the entertaining alongside the majestic and ethereal.

In addition to those sculptural motifs belonging to Cornwall,
churches in Burnard's locality often display more universally-known
formats, found all over England and Germany — that of the two
kneeling figures facing each other across a prayer-desk. This became
a fashionable type of monument for seventy years, and was used in
the seventeenth-century by most well-to-do Cornish families —
moulded in plaster and slate. Burnard must have seen just such a
tomb in North Hill church: the memorial to Henry Spoure, 1688.
The father and mother are kneeling opposite each other with the
children standing in niches behind. All four figures are realistically
coloured, and present an impressive unity within the standing wall-
monument with its columns, and its elaborate entablature and
pediment. This is an unusually conservative church monument,
being of the Elizabethan or Jacobean standing type. This type was
continued even into the eighteenth century, since the Classical
style arrived late in Cornwall.

Thus when Burnard looked around him he had fine precedents and
models to draw upon: sculpture and buildings which ably
expressed both the universal and the particular.

Early Employment at Fowey

Burnard's first employment in a sculptural capacity was at Place
House, Fowey, the seat of the Treffry family. Place comprises a
compact whole with the fourteenth-century church standing south-
east of it. Situated on a rise overlooking town and harbour, the
house originated in the fifteenth century. With its high battlemented
walls, towers, bays and greenery it is an impressive sight, and lives
up to its name — 'Place' signifying a palace.

The early sixteenth-century bay-window in the courtyard is the
most impressive feature — worked no doubt by the masons later
engaged on Launceston church, it shows a wealth of detail with its
grotesques, portraits, leaves and other motifs. It is two-storeyed with
transoms and with arched lights. The elaborate bay of the east front
was originally on the south side, and was re-erected with old materials.
Burnard was one of the band of masons under Whale of Altarnun,
whose job was to replace the south window with a more ornate and
striking bay. Attempts were made to copy the rich detail of the
adjacent Elizabethan bay. However, despite laborious working of
leaves, heads and shields, the animation of the earlier window could
not be repeated and the result was rather more stiff and awkward.

24

The intention of Joseph Thomas Treffry was virtually to rebuild Place, with the usual early Victorian obsession with gothic display. The 'repairs' of Place between 1813 and 1845 comprised building the impressive towers, an entrance hall of the finest polished specimens of porphyry, jasper and porphyritic granite; and a staircase mingling Georgian with Gothic details. Pevsner said about Place that it portrays an 'ambitious and somewhat elephantine Walter Scottian Romanticism.' Burnard certainly came into contact with a giant of Victorian industrialist ambition in the personage of Joseph Treffry, who was creating the thriving port of nearby Par, and starting up the silver and lead smelting works there. He built the railway to his granite quarries and was responsible for the magnificently-designed viaduct at Luxulyan. He owned rich mines in the district, and built a railway to Newquay, which he intended to become a commercial port on the North Coast of Cornwall. Treffry seems to have taken to the ambitious fifteen-year-old Burnard with his brawny stature and round face. Burnard later persuaded him to provide a valuable pedestal of porphyry, jasper and amethyst for his marble bust of the young Prince of Wales for the Polytechnic Society; he obviously knew how to get round Treffry. In a letter to Mr. Rundle in 1847 he said that in order to get the porphyry he would 'Take him when he's in the humour', and suggested there would be an inscription on the pedestal to the effect that Treffry had donated it in honour of the Queen's visit to his house. Burnard later executed a bust of Treffry, now in the entrance hall of Place.

As to Burnard's personal work on the house itself, it is impossible to be specific. It is stated by Hamilton Davey that he 'carved in stone and modelled in plaster a number of medallions and other decorations.' However, Mrs. Ann Treffry of Place was unable to find more than a few particular references to Burnard in the relevant documents belonging to the mansion. Probably he assisted with the motifs on the south bay.

Working with painters, decorators and specialists in a variety of stone must have been a valuable experience for Burnard. He was also in the midst of a stately home which incorporated many decorative styles; from Elizabethan plasterwork, oak-panelling and heraldic chimney-pieces, to the High Victorian lavishness of detail. He met here influential people who enjoyed being patrons of promising young artists; and his own reading and drawing were laying strong foundations for his future career.

Fowey church doubtless brought additional established styles to Burnard's notice. Rededicated in 1336, the tower comprises four stages and buttresses, and its profuse decoration is reminiscent of that on Launceston church. There is a plinth with two strips of decoration: the first string course has two strips of ornament, the second and third string courses also have two bands. The pinnacles are sculpted in relief against the top parts of the buttress; they are panelled and the battlements are ornamented. The interior seems inspired by friars' architecture, in that there are no capitals on the piers ; simply a smooth sweep. The Norman font is of delicate workmanship : it is of black Catacleuse stone with encircled rosettes, and an upper-border of crossed zig-zag lines. Also in the church is a remarkable recumbent statue to John Rashleigh, surmounted by two cherubs representing his grandsons who predeceased him. The young Burnard must have been impressed by the excellence of this workmanship, as he would have been by those of the Spoure and Vincent memorials at North Hill.

In Fowey Church, Burnard undertook to carve a white marble plaque fixed on a slate to Elizabeth Willcocks, who died in 1835 aged 36. He signed it ' N. N. Burnard, Sculpt-Altarnun' The motif sculpted seems to be a branch of myrtle, bay or laurel with berries on the right of the inscription, but unberried on the left. The oval bears incised lettering which is simple and refined ; around its top is a draped curtain carved in relief.

Another admirer of Burnard was the novelist Sir Arthur Quiller-Couch, who wrote of his much-loved Fowey in ' Troy Town ' and ' The Mayor of Troy'. ' Q ' thought highly of Burnard's capacities for writing in verse ; he had heard many favourable accounts of Burnard from his father, T. Q. Couch of Bodmin.

Probably whilst he was at Fowey Burnard carved the three shields which appear on the facade of the National Schools at Tywardreath. He could always turn his hand to any sort of technique, whether it was low relief and heraldic, geometric design, or sculpture in the round. In carrying out this task he may well have been consciously referring back to the heraldic and decorative flat panels, contemporary with the seventeenth-century slates in church embellishment.

London : A Royal Commission

After his introduction to Sir Francis Chantrey, who was very much taken with his honesty and lowly birth (he had been a milk-boy himself), Burnard was employed in London as a carver with Henry Weekes. Weekes had trained as Chantrey's assistant and held the professorship of Sculpture at the Royal Academy — he sculpted, amongst many other works, the tomb bust of Charles Buller in Westminster Abbey. Weekes died in 1877 at the age of seventy. After working with Weekes, Burnard went on to help and learn in Chantrey's studio as well as in other celebrated ateliers. He helped Chantrey with his best works, as well as receiving commissions from famous sculptors like Baily, Marsh and Foley. By 1841 Burnard could confidently exhibit at the Polytechnic, as an independent sculptor with a studio and an already well-advanced reputation.

The sculpture which established his claim to fame and brought numerous commissions was that of the six-year-old Prince of Wales, later King Edward VII. It was through his first patron, Sir Charles Lemon, that Burnard was introduced to Queen Victoria as an able sculptor for the subject of her son. His efforts were finally rewarded by the information that ' Her Majesty and Prince Albert thought it very correct.' This bust was exhibited at Falmouth Polytechnic Society ; much acclaimed, it was bought by public subscription. The portrait became widely known ; it always epitomized, even if indirectly, Burnard's own reputation. The Western Independent newspaper of October 6th, 1929, published an article entitled ' A Wayward Cornish Genius — Neville Northy Burnard. From Royal Palace to Pauper's Grave.' Headlines suitably momentous to attract closer attention.

The Lander Statue and Truro

Despite the fact that most of Burnard's portraits were executed in marble, his early love for stone and the lessons he learnt from monumental stone-carvers were expressed in a four-ton statue, which was erected at the top of Lemon Street, Truro, in 1852. It is probably the finest work he did both in scale and composition. Burnard's desire to perpetuate his own memory and that of a fellow-Cornishman is evident by the gusto with which he threw himself into the arduous task.

Richard Lander of Truro had pursued Mungo Park's discovery of the Niger by tracing its course through some thousand miles of unexplored country to the sea. He had been shot in an ambush on the Brass River and died on February 7, 1834, at Fernando Po. A Doric column was erected in Lemon Street, Truro, by the deaf and dumb architect Mr. Sambell, and the intent was to place Lander's statue on it. It was not until 1849 that sufficient funds enabled Burnard to be entrusted with the work of modelling Lander. On March 12th the Royal Cornwall Gazette reported that the statue was cut from magnesium limestone and stood ten feet high. The report marvelled at the novel aspect of the head, inclining towards the spectator instead of looking into vacancy. Lander is in modern costume with loose trousers and frock coat. There are symbolic accoutrements of the explorer: the palm-branch he holds signifies his peaceful mission in Africa ; the right arm leans on an elegant pedestal which bears the heads of a hippopotamus and a crocodile, so common in the Niger (modelled at Regent's Park Zoo). There are bull-rushes, tropical leaves and wave-like motifs to represent water. A map lies on the pedestal and marks the course Lander followed. The fourth side bears a large straw sun-hat and portmanteau. All these things lend the figure both physical and compositional support. Apparently it is a good likeness, but was, in fact, laboriously achieved by combining the features of Lander's daughter with a portrait from the Royal Geographical Society.

Standing as it does, some seventy feet from the ground at the top of Lemon Street where it joins the Falmouth Road, the statue is truly impressive, and is in perfect harmony with the classicism of the street. (Illustrations 40-42).

Burnard's appreciation of classical simplicity was certainly encouraged by his associations with Chantrey's circle and the neo-classicism of contemporary English sculpture. But when he first went to London he was no stranger to Georgian architecture. Truro is one of those Cornish towns of rich elegance, with town mansions not unlike those of Bath and Bristol. Built in the mid-eighteenth century, those houses between Boscawen Street and Quay Street are plain outside with their wrought-iron palings — inside there are great staircases, halls, plaster-ceilings and walls. These were all homes of those merchants who had profited by the huge boom in mineral ores (commodities in which Cornwall was so fantastically wealthy). Burnard took the delightful Georgian aspect of Lemon Street into account when he carved the Lander statue. Built in 1795, Lemon Street is of plain, granite-faced two-and three-storeyed houses ascending northwards to the Doric column and the Greek-style church of St. John (1827-28). Its pavement kerb stones are great granite blocks. This street was the wonder of Cornwall, and its grandeur is echoed through Truro in the Georgian crescent of Walsingham Place and the granite Market Hall by Christopher Eales. The Royal Institution museum, in River Street, which houses Burnard''s fine bust of Richard Trevithick and the portrait of Catherine Enys, is itself another classical building.

'The Builder' in its report on March 27th, 1852, gave a favourable report of the Lander work; Burnard later won a competition for placing a statue of Ebenezer Elliott, the Corn-Law Rhymer in the Market Square, Sheffield. Thus his first full-length statue in Cornwall stood Burnard in good stead for obtaining similar commissions, proving him to be an artist capable of monumentality as well as refinement of detail and nuance.

Despite the importance of all the foregoing influences exerted upon Burnard within Cornwall, it cannot be denied that London was responsible for broadening his education and giving him purpose, contacts and a business-like practicality. He early made the friendship of the painter G. F. Watts, who conducted him around the metropolis, and who helped to direct the sculptor's energies into the correct and useful channels. In the various ateliers of sculptors Burnard now learnt much and practised hard, copying and studying from the works of masters old and new.

FOUR

BURNARD AND CHANTREY

The years in London

In London Burnard must have become more aware of the long tradition of sculpture into which he was gradually being drawn. It is important to understand something of the sculpture which came before the nineteenth century, because Burnard was part of the developing tradition, and so may be said to have contributed towards our heritage in a minor way.

Around 1600 the main fields for sculptors were in providing church-memorials and portrait-busts. (Burnard worked within this convention in his memorial-busts of George Smith and Hugh Rogers). There was additional employment for eighteenth-century sculptors in the big houses, carving marble chimney-pieces. Immigrant continental trends seem to have called the tune in Britain after the Restoration and into the eighteenth-century. During the reign of George II, sculpture commissions seem to have been in the hands of three foreign-born sculptors. The first two were Scheemakers (1691-1781) and Rysbrack (1694-1770), both from Antwerp. Their works include a marble bust of George II, a standing Locke, and a reclining Newton. Louis François Roubiliac (1705?-1762), was the third artist, one of those surrounding Hogarth. His statue of Handel, set up in the Pleasure Gardens at Vauxhall in 1738 (now in the Victoria and Albert Museum), has been acclaimed as a landmark in the history of English Rococo.

Roubiliac's penetrating sculpture of Alexander Pope is a wonder in its characterization. His style was followed well into the nineteenth century. In 1847 we find Burnard writing to Mr. Rundle that: 'The Earl of Falmouth wants a marble bust of Admiral Boscawen executed from the plaster model by Roubiliac.'

In London, Burnard had the opportunity of studying the expressive busts of past sculptors like Joseph Wilton and Houdon. There were the precedents of Joseph Nollekens, (1737-1823); of John Gibson, (died in 1866); and Samuel Haydon, who died in 1891. Thomas Banks (1735-1805) was one of the first English sculptors to work in the neo-classic style. The study of his works may well have imparted to Burnard's best portraits some of their timeless quality and serenity. John Bacon (1771-1859) may have taught Burnard how and when to use detail and fine touches. One of his sculptures, to Guilieme Mason, the poet, is in Westminster Abbey.

Several of Burnard's contemporaries, in whose studios he often worked as apprentice, were famed for their grandiose schemes. A typical sculptor who lived and died famous was John Henry Foley (1818-1874). He was elected R.A. in 1858; he sculpted the Group of Asia, and the figure of Prince Albert for the Albert Memorial in

Kensington Gardens. He exhibited forty-nine works at the Royal Academy and lies buried at St. Paul's, after leaving the bulk of his property to the Artists' Benevolent Fund.

But it was his companionship and study with Francis Chantrey which must have made strongest impressions on Burnard. Chantrey could well understand the struggles of an artist of poor connections. He had been born near Sheffield in 1781; his father was a carpenter, and he started as a milk-boy and carver's apprentice. Eventually he succeeded as a bust portrait sculptor in London, as well as undertaking many other subjects in stone. He sculpted the equestrian statue of George IV in Trafalgar Square. Chantrey was elected full member of the R.A. in 1818, and after his return from France and Italy in 1819 he produced his finest works. Like Burnard, he possessed a native intelligence and wit which enabled him to make a large fortune. Chantrey may well have imprinted upon Bernard's mind the necessity for a business-like approach in art at that time. Burnard's letters to Mr. Rundell (the secretary of the Polytechnic Society) are full of ambitious projects to aid his own good reputation: to reproduce his works in plaster casts, or to draw attention to his name by a paragraph in the local papers entitled 'Local Intelligence'. Altogether, this professionalism in both the execution and positioning of his work doubtless contributed to Burnard's early success, as it did to Chantrey's.

Chantrey had the incentive to build his own foundry in Eccleston Place. He was devoted to shooting and fishing, was renowned for rough manners and strong language, but his hospitality was legendary. George Jones, his friend and biographer, wrote that Chantrey considered that the defects in England and the foreign schools arose from artists' attempts at picture-making — at drawing the attention by accurate detail or small parts; he thought the more essential points in art had not concerned the mind or feeling of the artist. He was continually talking of Leonardo's imagination and concentration on expression. In his biography of Chantrey, Jones cited Gibbon's *Decline and Fall* (Vol. ii, p.51).

'Sculpture, and above all, painting, propose to themselves the imitation not only of the forms of nature, but, of the characters and passions of the human soul. In these sublime arts, the dexterity of the hand is of little avail, unless it is animated by fancy, and guided by the most correct taste and observation.'

Jones wrote that Chantry
'. . . . liked to see ability rewarded and would willingly exert himself to this end: and often, when his words were ineffective, his purse contributed a compensation; from his early career his disposition led him to encourage rising artists — his generous nature induced him to excuse their defects and strongly recommend the beauties of their works.'

This encouragement of lesser-known artists was followed by Burnard. A letter to Rundell he wrote concerned finding a painter for Sir Charles Lemon's portrait, and suggested one who '. . . would give universal satisfaction, and at the same time be much benefited by the chance of getting such a commission.' The artist was, in fact, R. Whale of Altarnun (1805-87), who afterwards established a reputation as a portrait and landscape painter, and became an A.R.A. There are some good works of his at Nanscawen, Luxulyan, adjoining Prideaux, where he stayed before emigrating to America.

Chantrey emulated Turner and his work. His own busts appear to have a soft, fleshy quality, but they are also dignified by his sympathy with the antique. A man of his time, Chantrey must have engendered in Burnard his own enthusiasm for all aspects of human creativity. He had accumulated considerable skills as painter, draughtsman, architect, mechanic, and his interests lay in geology, chemistry and optics as well as the exact sciences. He must have had a physical resilience equal to Burnard's own, for he loved to relate instances of his early strength in mowing an acre of grass, thrashing a quarter of corn, or ploughing an acre, each in a day. Chantrey never hesitated in displaying his bluntness. Caroline Fox wrote of a story Burnard told her in 1847, 'Chantrey, after sustaining a learned conversation with Lord Melbourne to his extremest limits, saved his credit by "Would your Lordship kindly turn your head on the other side and shut up your mouth." '

Undoubtedly Chantrey encouraged Burnard to mix with a new company, one which could benefit him in his study, mental education and commissions. He obtained personal contacts with the intellectuals of a great period in British history: people sitting to him included William Ewart Gladstone, Dickens and Thackeray, Richard Cobden, John Couch Adams, John Bright and prominent members of the Geological Society — G. B. Greenhough and Professor E. Forbes.

Some Famous Portraits

Thomas Carlyle, the Scottish historian and essayist, took great interest in Burnard's progress. Burnard forwarded a note to Caroline Fox which he had received from Carlyle concerning a bust of the poet Charles Buller. 'Feb. 25, 1849 . . . Courage! Persist in your career with manful, patient and unquenchable endeavour, and if there lies a talent in you (as I think there does), the gods will permit you to develop it yet.' (See Appendix A.)

In the years he spent in London, Burnard's chisels moulded the features of the illustrious men of nineteenth-century science, religion, literature, art, astronomy and politics. But with his sympathetic impulsiveness he was not merely a detached spectator; soon he was drawn into the politics of the Chartist movement. In 1849 Ebenezer

Elliott, the 'Corn-Law Rhymer', hymn-writer and poet of the Hungry Forties, died. Burnard was moved to write a dirge addressed to 'Toilers' which was published in the 'West Briton', 1852:

'The poor hath lost a champion and a guide
One who could teach them to be truly free...'   (Appendix A.)

His statue of Elliott for Sheffield has already been mentioned. In 1858 he exhibited a bust of the poet at the Academy entitled 'The Corn-Law Rhymer'. Mr. L. Maker of Callington possessed some original letters written by Burnard; one of them, sent to a member of the Elliott statue committee, reads:

'I am a great admirer of Elliott and one of 'the people' who ought to be grateful to him. I am also ambitious that my name may be associated with such a lustrous name as his and I am sure you cannot blame me for this .... I only wish to have this lasting opportunity of showing that my love for the poet of the poor has somewhat of reality in it.'   (Appendix A.)

Burnard also sculpted in marble the hand of Richard Cobden (1804-65): the man who agitated with Bright for the abolition of tax on imported corn. The hand rests on an open Bible, pointing to the words: 'Give us this day our daily bread'.

In 1853, the year after the publication of 'Uncle Tom's Cabin,' Harriet Beecher Stowe visited London. Burnard's bust of her was proudly subscribed by the Anti-Slavery cause and put in the Crystal Palace at Sydenham. The Cornishman was often much involved in London's concerns, and in the lives and actions of the people he sculpted. His intellect and social standing increased in the capital. But having known great notorieties, he could never resist the occasional election squib, and was forever entertaining his hosts in Cornwall with descriptive anecdotes and wide-ranging topical discussion.

However, there was for him a considerable rival intellectual establishment to that of London, one at which Cornishmen of any promise or public merit were readily entertained: Penjerrick House, near Falmouth, Cornwall. Here the famous Quaker Fox family provided an incentive for Burnard to visit Cornwall and find Cornish commissions.

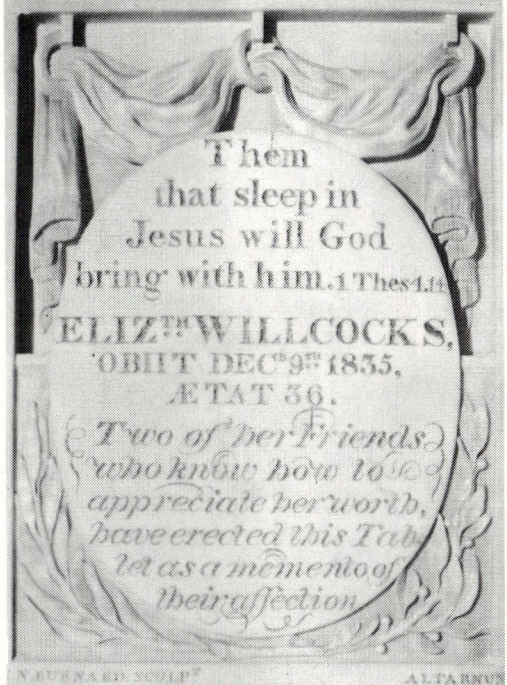

33 Burnard's marble memorial in Fowey Church, executed during his employment at Place House.

34 The south bay of Place House, constructed by Altarnun masons, including the young Burnard.

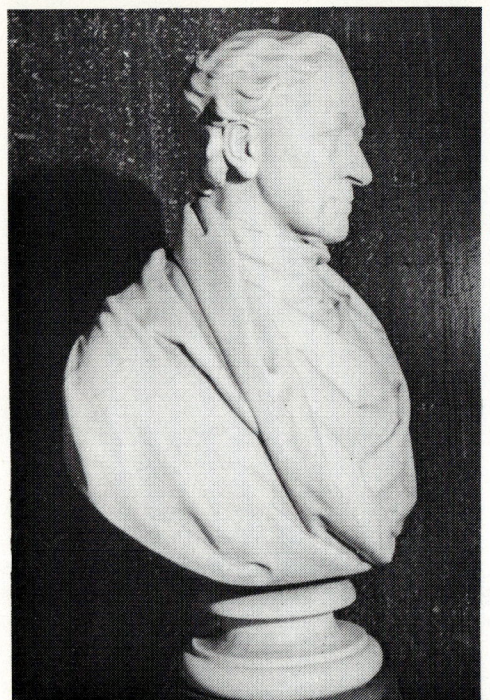

35 Bust of Joseph Thomas Treffry, in Place House, executed by Burnard at the height of his powers.

36 Tombstone to James Whitburn (Gwennap Church), carved by Burnard, aged 15.

37 Marble bust of the Prince of Wales
(later Edward VII) : a royal commission
for Burnard (in Polytechnic Hall,
Falmouth).

38 Medallion portrait of Mrs. Catherine
Enys (in Truro Museum).

39   Marble bust of Richard Trevithick
       (in Truro Museum).

40   Statue of Richard Lander, upper
Lemon Street, Truro : erected in 1852.

BURNARD'S CORNISH ASSOCIATIONS

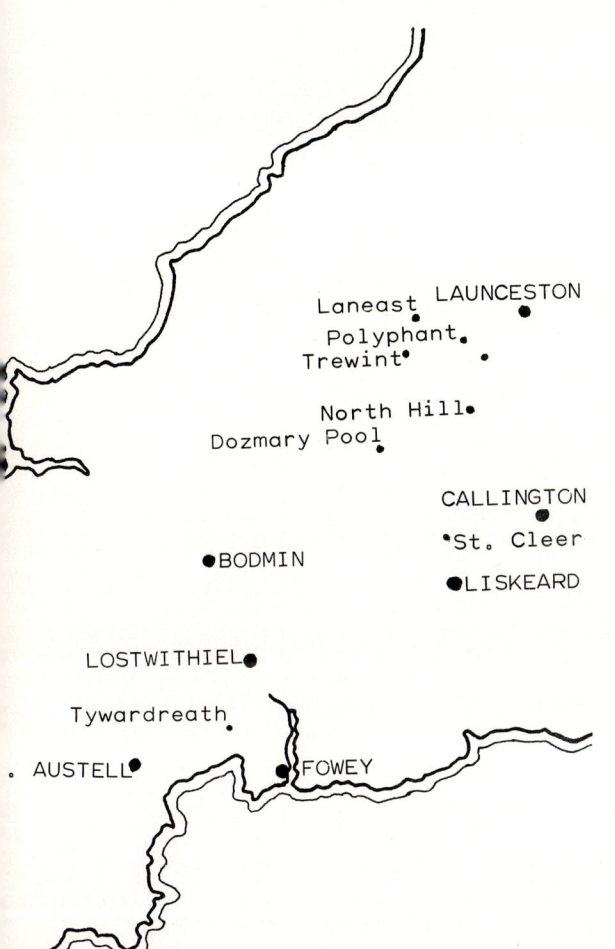

Laneast
LAUNCESTON
Polyphant
Trewint
North Hill
Dozmary Pool
CALLINGTON
St. Cleer
BODMIN
LISKEARD
LOSTWITHIEL
Tywardreath
AUSTELL
FOWEY

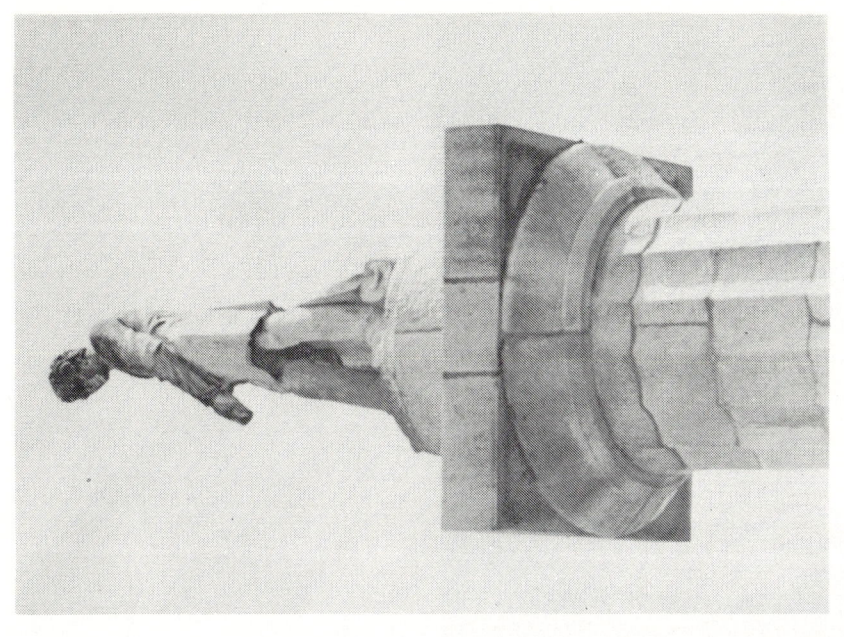

41-42 Statue of Richard Lander, upper Lemon Street, Truro : erected in 1852.

43 Bust of Richard Lander, reputedly
by Burnard.

44 Dr. William Borlase : plaster bust
(in Truro Museum).

45   Portrait of an unknown gentleman, by Burnard (pencil : in Truro Museum).

46   Portrait of Rev. William Rowe, Vicar of St. Teath (pencil : in Truro Museum).

IN MEMORY OF
GEORGE SMITH,
OF TREVU, J.P. FOR THE COUNTY OF CORNWALL
L.L.D, F.A.S, &c. &c.
BORN 1800, DIED 1868.
AUTHOR OF THE HISTORY OF WESLEYAN METHODISM
"SACRED ANNALS" AND OTHER WORKS,
HE WAS A MEMBER OF THIS SOCIETY 47 YEARS.

47   Burnard's memorial to Dr. George Smith, in Wesley Church, Camborne.

FIVE

PENJERRICK: AN INTELLECTUAL CENTRE IN CORNWALL

The Fox Family

The Foxes of Falmouth were one of those families in Cornwall who took it upon themselves to find and nourish local talent. It was to this end that Anna Maria and Caroline (the two daughters of the house) started in 1833 the Cornwall Polytechnic Society — the establishment where (it may be recalled) Burnard acquired his early fame. Others in Cornwall similarly dedicated were the Gilbert and Lemon families. It was Davies Gilbert, later President of the Royal Society, who helped Humphry Davy (inventor of the miner's safety lamp) and Richard Trevithick (inventor of the high-pressure steam engine). Sir Charles Lemon, first president of the Polytechnic Society and a regular guest at the Foxes', certainly did a great deal for Burnard by way of introductions.

For many years Penjerrick had been a Mecca for all who had been in the public eye. It was set amid extensive semi-tropical gardens in the healthy mild climate of Falmouth; its calm and hospitality provided a stimulating and recuperative atmosphere. The Foxes' intelligence and delight in learning brought the friendship of men like Carlyle and Charles Kingsley. Anna Maria and Caroline, around whom much of the conversation revolved (as in the days of the salons), were fortunate in that their father held high rank in scientific fields. But they themselves possessed keen intellects which attracted men like Wordsworth, Derwent Coleridge, Fred D. Maurice, Guizot, Chevalier Bunsen, John Stuart Mill, John Sterling, Sir Henry de la Beeche, Professor John Couch Adams, Sir Edward Sabine and Dr. Gladstone. In its annual Report, the Royal Cornwall Polytechnic Society, of which Anna Maria was virtually the founder, summed up the secret of her winning personality:

'All who knew her could see that a deep and strong religious faith was the mainspring of her life's activities, yet bigotry and ascetic gloom found no place in her sunny and joyous character.'

Far from being a place where witticisms were bandied about and cynicisms exchanged, Penjerrick was a haven of Quaker tolerance, openness, humility and intelligence; Caroline Fox's Journals readily convey these qualities in the conversations she reported. It was in this spirit of simplicity and amiability that Burnard was so enthusiastically received. Caroline Fox's Journals contain interesting accounts of meetings with him. Born 24 May, 1819, she kept up her diary of letters which was eventually published under the title 'Memories of Old Friends'. In 1847, Burnard was invited to

Penjerrick in connection with his exhibit at the Polytechnic show. Miss Fox wrote: 'He is a great, powerful, pugilistic-looking fellow, at twenty-nine; a great deal of face, with all the features massed in the centre; mouth open, and all sorts of simplicities flowing out of it . . .'

No doubt the Foxes as well as his later listeners were fascinated by Burnard's personal renderings of the 'inside life of the greats.' The description of his visit continues: 'His stories of Chantrey very odd. On his death Lady Chantrey came into the studio with a hammer and knocked off the noses of many completed busts, so that they might not be too common — a singular attention to her departed lord.'

Burnard and Couch Adams

John Couch Adams, the Cornish astronomer, also came to Penjerrick. Both he and Burnard visited within five days of each other; it may well have been at Caroline's suggestion that Burnard sculpted a bust of Adams. In fact, Couch Adams and Burnard were neighbours by birthplace; and the similarities of their early years are quite remarkable. Adams' home was Lidcot, a small farm in Laneast, the parish just an hour's walk from Altarnun. The eldest of seven children of Thomas Adams and Tabitha Knill Grylls, John was born in 1819, less than a year after Burnard. His people had been farmers for generations in the Laneast area, always active in parish affairs and the local Wesleyan Society. The impossibility of having enough money to send the promising young John to Cambridge was actually overcome, for a rich deposit of manganese was found on the farm and, together with a small bequest his mother inherited, the necessary cash was raised for his education at St. John's College, Cambridge. Adams' idea of the reversed method of reasoning (i.e. from an unknown to a known) led him to become one of the discoverers of the planet Neptune. In 1848 the Royal Society awarded him the Copley Medal, and he was elected President of the Astronomical Society in 1851.

Caroline Fox spoke well of Adams after meeting him at Carclew for dinner. She finally penetrated his shyness by getting him to speak on his best-loved subject to her. She learnt that he sent his mathematical evidence for the reason for Uranus' disturbances to Airy, the Royal Astronomer. Airy, indignant that an unknown should presume to strike out such a revolutionary path in mathematical science, locked Adams' papers up. Thus it was the Leverriers' simultaneous discovery of Neptune which was published first and given the credit. But Caroline Fox wrote:

'Professor Adams speaks of those about whom the English scientific world is so indignant, in a spirit of Christian philosophy, exactly in keeping with the mind of a man who had discovered a planet, and with warmest admiration of Leverrier.'

And again October 8:

'Professor Adams' talk yesterday did me great good, showing in living clearness how apparent anomalies get included and justified in a larger Law. There are no anomalies, and I can wait until all the conflicts of Time are reconciled in the Love and Light of Heaven.'

The passage above exemplifies the atmosphere of scientific discovery and Christian strength with which Burnard came into contact at Penjerrick. Undeniably this was the acme of the many circles he moved in, whether fashionable, or, as in the case of the Dawe family at Crow's Nest, humble and isolated from society.

Despite more London commissions than he could cope with, Burnard's special interest lay in portraying Cornish people. His busts include those of Sir Charles Lemon, Dr. William Borlase, Charles Buller (1806-48, buried in Westminster Abbey with a portrait bust sculpted by Burnard's first master — H. Weekes), Richard Trevithick, Admiral Boscawen ; and Mary Kelynack, the fish wife from Newlyn who walked all the way to London to see the Great Exhibition, and was received by Queen Victoria.

SIX

LATER YEARS

Marriage and the Death of Lottie

Of Burnard's marriage and years in London little is known. At the height of his fame he married Mary Ann Nicholson. She was apparently from an artistic family, for in a letter Burnard mentions that he planned to bring on a visit to Cornwall a 'very talented artist . . . a true Cockney' — his brother-in-law, who was sculptor, etcher, glyphographer and lithographer. The house and street in which Burnard lived, 36 Hugh Street, Pimlico, no longer exist. Neville and Ann had two sons and two daughters, and appear to all accounts to have been happy. His son, Thomas Burnard, exhibited at the Royal Academy between 1868 and 1886. He was resident at the same address and sculpted busts of the following:

1868   The late Sir Charles Lemon, Bart, F.R.S. (medallion).
1869   Medallion portrait
1879   Richard Baxter, Esq.
1886   William McDonald Sinclair, M.A. (bust).

Inexplicably, Neville Burnard's concentration started to drift in his fifties. He grew unsettled, left his wife, drank often and neglected his work. On the death of his eleven year old daughter Lottie, his restlessness became pervaded with a sense of empty futility and rebellion against the conventional society of which he had been a member for thirty years. (See Appendix C.)

At this time he wrote these verses:

NOT DEAD BUT SLEEPING

As calm and beautiful in death she lay
We gazed on her that from our hearts was reft,
And saw the Robber, faltering in his theft
Had stolen the fire but not the charms away,
For, that was there the Spoiler could not slay,
That dared the venom of his deadliest shaft,
That branch of Life heaven's Gardner doth engraft
On earth's frail plants that wither in a day.

Still on that face our inmost souls ador'd
Reposed a child-like half celestial smile
As if to heaven or earth, in little while
She might be wafted or again restored ;
As if, in crossing Death's mysterious ford
She midway rested on some happy isle.

Gone! like some pure, benignant spirit of light,
　Who, on his way to some unclouded star,
　That men might see how fair the angels are,
Slacken'd, a space, the swiftness of his flight.

They saw his god-like mien, his robes of white,
　His rapid pinions' iridescent dyes,
　And the mild lustre of his gracious eyes,
When, lo! he soar'd, sublimely, out of sight.

Even so *our* angel paus'd a little while,
　On her great journey through the awful vast,
　And on our humble hearth a glory cast ;
Gave us to see a face unknown to guile,
Spake some dear words, and with a heavenly smile,
To Him ' that maketh perfect all things ' pass'd.

A Dream

Last night I dream'd that I and Lottie stroll'd,
　At the sweet, tender hour of eventide,
　Adown the meads with Spring's sweet firstlings pied,
As in the dear, delightful days of old.

Near us the mighty Thames majestic roll'd,
　The wind scarce whispering 'mid his fringe of reeds,
　And all things seem'd informed with that which feeds
The mind with thoughts too sacred to be told.

Though weak and infantile her accents were
　Deep wealth of words my eager ears beguiled ;
　She knew of what the birds were warbling wild,
And could the secrets of the flowers declare.
　' Art thou,' I cried, ' an Angel or a Child?'
When straight she blended with the odorous air.

Return to Cornwall

Burnard closed his studio and travelled westward to Cornwall.
From then on he found temporary respites in the homes of childhood
friends and East Cornwall workmen. He lived by writing political
lampoons or poetry for local newspapers, and made pencil and
pen sketches of local worthies in return for a night's lodging. The
mass of his verse seems uninspired and unmemorable, but he was,
rarely, able to achieve a lyrical quality, particularly when writing of

his beloved daughter. The above are moving because they are simply felt and genuine, with a touching faith and lack of bitterness. Most of his rhyming effort seems wasted on jingoistic witticisms, though often these are amusing. Once, whilst in a Liskeard inn, Burnard handed a note containing the following rhyme to a farmer called Nicoll, whom he had sketched and who had taken the sketch without paying:

> ' Cash is scarce, and fortune's fickle
> I should like to draw some silver now
> As I've all day been drawing nickel.'

However, at times, he forgot his misery, loss and sour disillusionment. He was able to draw attention with his brilliant personality, his entertaining accounts of the famous people he had met, and his stirring rendering of passages from Shakespeare and Burns. He contributed the following to the Poet's Corner of the West Briton newspaper:

> I owe a debt to Burn's name,
>   A debt which scarce a life can pay ;
>   I think with rapture of the day
> When I a worshipper became
>   Of that great soul which even now
>   Speaks to my spirit from the plough.
>
> Long time was Burns my sole delight,
>   With him I laugh'd, with him I wept ;
>   He lay beside me when I slept,
> At early dawn he cheer'd my sight ;
>   His manly spirit was my stay
>   Through every toil of every day.
>
> I found new charms in every flower,
>   And in the song of every bird,
>   A harmony till then unheard,
> Of sweet significance and power ;
>   And all the rocks and cliffs around
>   Did with new majesty abound.
>
> I walked as in a better land,
>   I spake as with a loosen'd tongue ;
>   And daily as to me he sung,
> I felt my sympathies expand ;
>   For, though not deem'd a churl before,
>   With him I loved mankind the more.

In poverty's familiar face,
   I now could charms abundant find ;
   I learnt with joy that in the mind
True wealth alone could find a place ;
   Led by his light, I first began
   To see the dignity of man.

(From ' Lines Written on the Celebration of the Birthday of Robert Burns '.)

Burnard at Crow's Nest

It was at this time that Burnard stayed with the Dawe family for some months ; he seems to have found understanding and temporary contentment with them at Crow's Nest, St. Cleer, near Liskeard. F. Hamilton Davey describes his arrival thus:

' Towards the close of 1875, he paid his first visit to the house of the late Mr. Dawe of Crow's Nest, St. Cleer. It was a dark, howling night, and with the exception of Mr. Dawe who was enjoying his pipe by the inglenook, the household had retired to bed. Amid the storm a knock was heard at the door. On opening it, Mr. Dawe was addressed in gentlemanly tones by a figure of titanic build, who craved a night's shelter. It proved to be Burnard, unkempt and tempest-worn. After being served with refreshment he commenced one of his entertaining chats, and on and on it went, until morning dawned without either the twain having sought his bed. Burnard stayed with the Dawes for over five months, and was not known to touch intoxicants during the whole of that time.'

The album, in which he wrote and drew and which he gave Harry Dawe and his family, is full of meticulous work and throws an interesting light on Burnard. Within the painstaking neatness of rows upon rows of verse lie wit and humour, sentimentality and regret, local jibes and acute sorrow. Altogether the album contains the jottings and leisured personal comments of a man not conscious of the public eye, but creating for his own amusement and that of the friends close to him. It is, therefore, a valuable record giving insight into Burnard's character and should not be judged according to aesthetic rules, as must his public work. Besides verse there are some delightful drawings in this book: sensitive pencil portraits of Harry Dawe and his daughters Maud, Gertie and Lizzie. There is the self-portrait (frontispiece) under which Burnard wrote: ' In self-defence I was compelled to draw.'

About this time most well-to-do families were collecting albums of photographic portraits of themselves. Burnard's drawings were intended to be a similar record ; his verses to Gertie Dawe at the front of the album include these scathing comments on a local barber who evidently had set up as a photographer:

' With us the photographic album now
Has grown to quite a family institution —
Matrons and maiden care not whence now how
They to their list can get a contribution,
Though they'll despise it if you don't impart
A picture large enough to fill a cart.
I was appealed to by Miss Gertie Dawe,
But as my phizz the barber had not taken
In self-defence I was compelled to draw —
The only chance I had to save my bacon ;
And gracious Gertie says my sketch, for fun done,
Pleases her more than any by the sun done.
Plain, plodding people shrink from looking dull,
Dread being taken to the very letter
Though they no more can change the face than skull
And look their worst in trying to look better,
Paying some barber for a facial sham
Instead of saying. ' Take me as I am.'
Turn, turn again these gilt-edge pages
And you'll endorse my bold asserveration
That the disease called egotism rages
Fiercest among the Lords of the Creation.
But howsoever their faults they try to gloss over
They never pass a dunce for a philosopher.

There is also a series of drawings of ladies in the dress of different historical periods ; under one are comments in the tiniest, most exquisite writing. These cameo drawings are of Lady Jane Grey, Matilda (wife of William the Conqueror), and ladies from the courts of Henry VI and Charles II. Also in the album are cameos of Hogarth, Benjamin Franklin, Washington, Wesley and Bunyan ; and the face of a young child in the village, whose early death caused Burnard heart-break as had his own daughter's loss. Underneath the dainty drawing of this little girl he has inscribed, ' A face that I could not Carrick-ature.' (The child's surname was Carrick.)

Also in the album appears another poem Burnard wrote in memory of his beloved Lottie :

Sonnet on Lottie's Birthday

May 29th, 1870

' This is her birthday — O that I might bring
As a sweet offering to our darling's tomb,
A garland cull'd from all the flowers that bloom
Throughout the fairest provinces of Spring!
If to celestials earthly memories cling,
Our thoughts of what she loved here while she stayed
Till her dear form was 'neath the violets laid

40

Might tempt her hitherward away to wing.
An angel whispers ' All the world of flowers
Father, is now unfolded to my sight —
Death did but fill the cup of my delight
And wake to endless life my latent powers.
Still am I yours, and will unseen requite
Your love with wreaths from amaranthine bowers.' '

Throughout the perusal of this album one grows aware of a conflict within Burnard, usually connected with drink. Certainly the household he stayed in was a restraining influence on this obsession of his ; during these months spent with the Dawes he scarcely touched alcohol. But in many of his rhymes there is that continual harping on the subject of drink, and of extremes being the cause of downfall ; implying that the fear of his own succumbing to his tendencies was always present. Many of the poems are humorous and facile, but often Burnard puts disproportionate blame and condemnation of local characters fond of indulging. It is as if he is foreseeing his own fate, and is subconsciously blaming his own weakness in despising others.

One such poem is ' A Village Hampden ', in which Burnard unleashes a fierce harangue upon farmer Venning — a brash sort of man who seems to have been in a continual state of fightable drunkenness at Altarnun. Burnard describes with a barbed humour the shameful ignorance and obstinacy of Venning when, bursting in upon a sermon in which the visiting preacher was extolling the greatness of the universe, he shouts out that the preacher is a liar to say that the earth is not flat. Venning is finally removed and with the verbal approval of Burnard is given a few ' fisticuffs ' outside to sober him him up ; but not until he has bellowed out — ' I beleev, I beleev the Zun goath round the Wurld.'

In a long poem of rhyming couplets, ' The Bibliomaniac ', Burnard again touches on the dangers of extreme behaviour, which so threatened him, as he secretly knew:

It is said of a good thing
One cannot have too much.
It's a foolish thought and
I'll prove it as such
There are scores of good things
Of which moderate use
Mental and physical welfare induce —
But go to extremes, and you'll certainly find
You have made a mistake in body and mind.
Indulge without stint, and I venture on oath
That you'll very soon find you are failing in both.

However, Burnard was far from being a self-righteous, puritanical kill-joy. He shows his rejection of the conventional brand

41

of Hell and Heaven-believing Methodists, by believing Hell to lie
within everyone and not as a separate place. He can rarely refrain
from poking fun at the clergy's pomposity or the prim and proper
morals of the families in his locality. In his poem 'Lines written
with an Old Scratchy Pen ', he describes a dream he had about the
Devil. He addresses it to the daughter of Mr. Dawe, Maud, in whose
room he (apologetically) finds the Devil in the form of a horribly
gruesome dog. He cannot think why the devil should be anywhere
near Maud, since she is always so blemishlessly good and innocent.
However, by talking to the Devil with the contempt he deserves,
Burnard finds him shrinking to pitiful dimensions. He then bids
Maud cut the Devil's claws to make his ignominy complete. In this
extract Burnard is addressing the Devil :

> If on business you came, you've mistaken the house ;
> The people out here aren't so easy to chouse.
> You don't want to mingle with sober exemplars,
> With Methodists, Total Abstainers, and Templars ;
> For here all the district is set against liquor
> With certain exceptions, including the vicar!
>
> Come, rouse thee ! or else the sleek brethren in black
> Will fancy they've nothing now left to attack.
> By the Devil is meant anything that is bad,
> In man, or in woman — in girl or in lad —
> 'Twill grow if encouraged, and shrink if opposed
> Its career in the presence of harmony's closed.
> If you're wishful to drive the old serpent away,
> Be gentle and generous, day after day . . .
> He doesn't like water, so stick to that tap
> And you'll soon be too strong for the fiery old chap.
> You'll see his old carcass get smaller and thinner
> If the publican finds he can't make you a sinner.
> Stick as firmly as Maud to the Temperance cause
> And you'll find there's no trouble in cutting his claws.

Certainly Burnard was adept at a number of verse forms ; he
delighted juggling around with visual poems, as in the following
piece, ' An Acrostic on Acrostics (Inscribed to Miss Gertie Dawe).' At
the top of this panel is a pen and ink drawing of a crow on a nest.
The initial letter in each line forms the name of the hamlet in
which he was staying.

> ' Acrostics as a general rule
> Construct and curb poetic diction,
> Reining the rhymer in — they cool
> Or place him 'neath undue restriction.
> Why should a free born bard be bound,

42

Strait-jacketed in flowery places,
Not having power to look around,
Even on the Muses, or the Graces.
Shunn'd be such stickling for first letters:
True poets cannot dance in fetters.'

He also wrote the following in the Dawes' album: a reminiscence of that time when he had sculpted the young Prince of Wales.

I rather like a wicked boy, provided
    He do not with his antics mingle malice ;
I've seen of harmless mischief a decided
    Example e'en in Queen Victoria's palace.
Though princes in all ages have prided
    Themselves upon their rank, their nature tallies
With ' poor humanities '; a Prince enjoys
    Frolic and fun as much as other boys.

In F. Hamilton Davey's Monograph on Burnard, published in 1911 from the Journal of the Royal Cornwall Polytechnic Society, is an account of how the mischievous six-year old Prince of Wales tricked Burnard (to whom he was sitting) into smelling some clay, and then pushed it up his nose. After being admonished, the Prince apologised: ' Sorry, Burnard — Won't do it again — Ma says I'm a donkey.'

Burnard was never above writing in dialect, and the effect of his words when read out loud is very much like listening to the broad lilt of a typical East Cornwall accent. In the following dialect poem, the main attractions of the parish of St. Cleer are described ; here is Burnard's explanation of the famous megalithic burial chamber, Trethevy Quoit.

Zum Coorossatees in Sencleer en Linkeyhorn. A Pome By a
Member o' theh Arternen Skulebored
Zum zay thet ondert thers eh soart a toom —
O zum gurt king thet wanted lots o room —
Zum zay et war eh Halter — zum declair
No swart o sackreefize was nevvur thair ;
I theenk mezel et ez eh kind o' tabel
Made bout thick time they built thek tour a Bable.

The album contains a fine drawing of the Trethevy Quoit and another of that stupendous natural formation of balanced granite boulders — the Cheesewring. There is also a strong drawing of the Cornish metaphysician Samuel Drew, and opposite it a 98-verse poem praising his character. These are two delicate tiny drawing which seem to touch on a surrealist quality. One is of a thumb with the knuckle exuding countless miniature heads and is entitled 'A seedy wart ' — maybe it is a pun on a ' Thumbnail ' sketch, or a local joke shared with the Dawe family. The other is of a briar pipe as smoked by Mr. Dawe, the bowl of which similarly exudes dozens of tinily drawn heads.

Death of Burnard

Three years after his stay at Crow's Nest Burnard, again on his wanderings, called at the White Hart Hotel at Camborne and was taken ill. Some days later he died at Redruth Workhouse on November 27, 1878. His burial was unmourned but for the masons who were restoring Camborne church.

Ironically his grave, unmarked for 76 years, is a mere stone's throw from one of his finest portrait memorials, cut at the peak of his career. On the inside of the north wall of Camborne Parish Church is a marble relief of the Reverend Hugh Rogers, B.A., born Nov. 20, 1780, died July 10, 1858. (See Illustration 69.)

The work, particularly in its arrangement of drapery, is very much in the style of the eighteenth century. It has a calm serenity, and something of the ' Smile of Reason ' with which Houdon endowed his famous marble of Voltaire. In Burnard's carving there is a beauty of expression and delicate strength in the fine nose, mouth and especially the eyes. The light touches on the eyelid give a poignancy which points to both the sitter's character and Burnard's compassionate understanding of humanity. The eyes are experienced, but kindly — benevolent and humorous ; it is an ascetic face but not austere in regard. One is aware that one is looking at an individual. Burnard's skill has combined an idealized monumental portrait with an astute character study.

The same is true of the medallion marble of Dr. George Smith (1800-68) in Wesley Chapel, Chapel Street, Camborne. The portrait of the Wesleyan mission worker, with raised eyes and positive jaw, is more energetic and out-going than the former. There is a general impression of confidence, hope and purpose, wonderfully conveyed by Burnard's rugged, contoured handling of the face and the simple definite folds around the neck. (Illustration 47.)

SEVEN

CONCLUSION

There was a tragic dualism in Burnard's nature which underlay his rise and fall 'from rags to rags'. The dynamic energy, individualism and obstinacy within his character were the driving forces of his career; they were also responsible for his self-inflicted abandonment and his repulsion from all he had so painstakingly earned. It was a characteristic single-mindedness and impulsiveness which drew Burnard back to the scenes of his early hopes and rise to fame — back to the climate which had fostered and excited in him a love for sculpture. This single-mindedness led him to realize his ambitions. It also brought him to his downfall; when grief through the loss of his daughter came to him he flung himself into it utterly. Despite his success, it is difficult to believe he was completely absorbed by the society scene.

Written in 1911, Hamilton Davey's verdict on Burnard is generous, though perhaps rather too full-blown and eulogistic for us today:

> 'Burnard was cast in such an ample mould that he rarely failed to arrest attention: tall, broad-shouldered, well-knit, with limbs of a giant, the head of a god, and the flashing eye of a man who knows the heart of humanity. He was the ideal of physical perfection. Had he cared he could have carved for himself a niche in the temple of fame by the side of the country's greatest sculptors.'

Burnard was a craftsman working within a long tradition of skilful stone-handling. As such his work was appreciated by lowly-born craftsmen and tradesmen, who saw no separation between the art and the craft of an object.

As a Cornishman well-grounded in the idea of the functionalism of sculpture, he benefited from a sound knowledge of the potentialities of slate and stone. But in addition to simply 'doing a craftsmanlike job' he was a creative artist, who had a sensitive grasp of the essentials in his sitters' characters.

It is this understanding of character, and his ability to transmit it in visual terms which raises Neville Northy Burnard above so many portrait sculptors, and makes his work accessible to any age. These attributes make the recent neglect of his work shameful and unjustifiable. One can only hope that future generations will treasure the heritage he has bequeathed to them, and guard it well.

APPENDIX A

LETTERS AND POEMS

Letter from Neville N. Burnard to Robert Hunt, Secretary of the Polytechnic Society, Falmouth, relating to damage done to his group ' Contentment' through rail transport.

7 Williams Street,
Hampstead Road,
London.
October 2nd, 1843.

My dear Sir,

I have received your note, and am sorry that my poor performance has met such an untimely fate, but now it is done we must make the best of it. I have been to the Great Western Station and stated all the particulars to the head clerk who informs me that the carriage in their books was entered at £1 0s. 5d. but they only charged as far as Devonport, and the other 8 shillings is from Devonport to Falmouth. With regard to the injury done the work he says that the people at the office must have had some notion that it was not "all right" from their having allowed you to unpack it previously to paying the carriage. He says that I must ascertain the amount of injury done to the work and the sum which was paid the man for repairing it, and it shall be paid me by the company; but I think the best way will be for the coach office in Falmouth, in *Cornish phrase* to "*cry quits,*" or to throw one against the other, thus I think dealing easily by them for, as it has been so mutilated, the amount of injury done to it and probably *to me* will if they insist on a *further settlement,* bring them in debt. So you may undertake to say on my behalf that my lowest charge for the damage done to the group is £1 10s. od. and if that will not satisfy them I will have the opinion of one of the most eminent London sculptors on the subject which will *make it more.* The nature of the contents of the box was stated on the cover, so there is no excuse for them on that score, and the amount of it all is this, my work has been *injured,* and I *expect to be paid,* and I have the authority of the Superintendant (or whatever he may be) for demanding it. I trust my dear Sir, that the accident has not rendered the work unfit for exhibition and that the *judges* will take into consideration the unfortunate state in which they have to see it. I wish I could have had the repairing of it; I *know* these Italians and they are mostly *bunglers* at repairing anything. I will make further arrangements about its carriage to London in my next, please to let me know my *doom* as soon as convenient to you and I should be very thankful for a paper at the same time. I suppose you received my letter this morning. I should have sent it along with the box but was too late for post.

I am dear Sir
Yours very truly,
N. N. Burnard.

From Thomas Carlyle to Burnard.

(relating to Burnard's desire to execute a sculpture of Charles Buller, the poet, from his death mask.)

Chelsea
25th February, 1849.

Dear Sir,

With much regret and with some surprise I have to answer that my application to Mrs. Buller has been entirely without effect and that there is no hope whatever in a new effort there. She considers the mask to belong as property, for the present at least, to Mr. Weeks, is impatient of any suggestion to the contrary, in brief, has such a feeling on the subject that especially in her present weak and afflicted state, it would be quite unsuitable to urge her farther on the subject, or even to speak to her of it again. My little project in your behalf, therefore has proved a total and hopeless failure, for which I am sorry enough if that could do any good.

How you are now to proceed I have no right to advise, but it seems to me there can be no good likelihood of your modelling a bust in these circumstances (for the picture itself is very imperfect and you never saw the original) so that perhaps it were well if you throw away no more labour on that matter as it now stands but give it up altogether till better opportunities offer. Mr. Weeks by keeping possession of the mask seems to me effectually to exclude all other artists from any fair chance at all beside him, on that particular subject. But there are other busts in this world to be modelled, likenesses to be hit when you can see the features you are to imitate ! Truly it would be wise to apply yourself to one of these, and leave this altogether till the conditions mend. Nay if the conditions never mend, and you cannot get that bust to do at all you may find (as often turns out in life) that it was better for you you did not. Courage ! Persist in your career with wise strength, with silent resolution, with manful patient unconquerable endeavour, and if there lie a talent in you (as I think there does) the gods will permit you to develop it yet without consulting the men or Weekses on the matter !

Believe me,
Yours very sincerely,
T. Carlyle.

Sonnet by N. N. Burnard

(from Laurence Maker's collection)

When I regard the petals of a flower
My thoughts O God of Love to Thee arise
Their faultless form, their fragrance and their dyes
Bespeak supreme beneficence and power.
What is humanity, that Thou shouldest dower
Its dwelling-place with wealth of countless gems,
That pale the sheen of regal diadems
And vie with Thy bright bow which spans the shower ?

Through them Thou givest us a high behest
To love and worship all things good and fair,
And tellest us that if Thy tender care
Doth cherish forms in fragile beauty dressed,
How surely clay whereon Thou hast impressed
Thine image shall Thy greater bounty share.

From Neville N. Burnard to J. Fowler, Esq.

36 Hugh St., Eccleston,
Pimlico.
January 2nd, 1851.

My dear Sir,
  If you are at this time in Sheffield you will most probably have heard that I have executed and sent to your house a small model of what seems to me to be the best memorial to the memory of your old friend Elliott, considering that the sum raised for the purpose is not what you expected it would have been. I need not tell you, who are an admirer of poets in general, that you naturally feel more pleasure in seeing some semblance of the men themselves than in looking on aught less closely associated with them which of course any other thing would be. *You* would rather look on a faithful representation of your old friend Pemberton than on the costliest work that had *only* been consecrated to his memory. The one must of course awaken feelings which from its very nature, the other could not. With regard to another very important point which ought not to be overlooked, the monument which I propose will outlast anything that is *not* made of bronze and granite, and will also appear as it was at first intended it should until the end, for even in brass the end will come *some* time. Sheffield is a smoky place, and a dark material would not be affected by it. But I need not trouble you with suggestions, the thing will be plain enough to you when you see the model. What I would wish to remind you of is that when I last saw you, you were kind enough

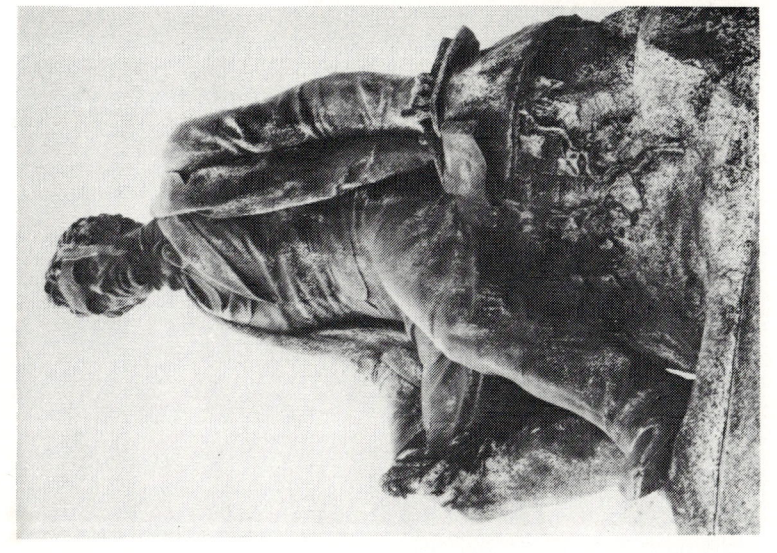

48-49 Statue of Ebenezer Elliott, the 'Corn Law Rhymer': 1854 (in Weston Park, Sheffield).

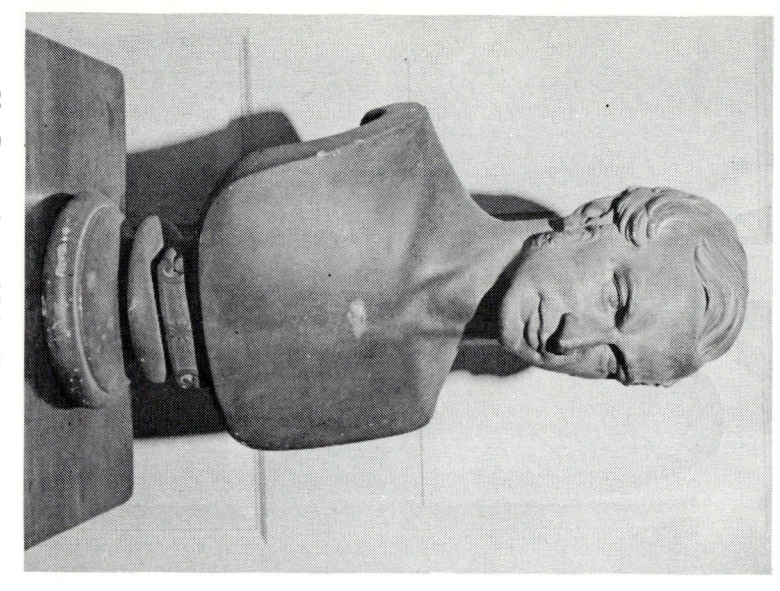

50 Bronze bust of John Couch Adams, astronomer, of Laneast.

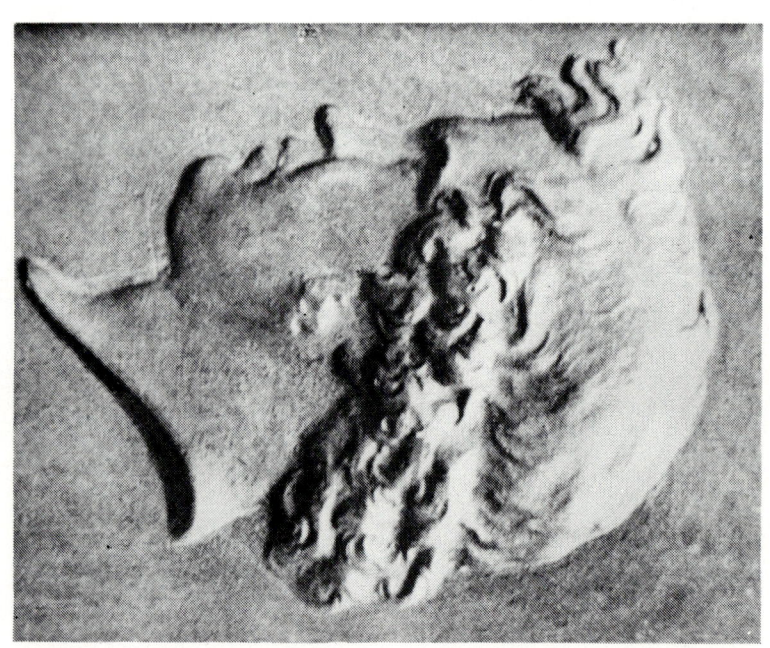

51 'A great, powerful, pugilistic-looking fellow' — Burnard's self-portrait, about 1850.

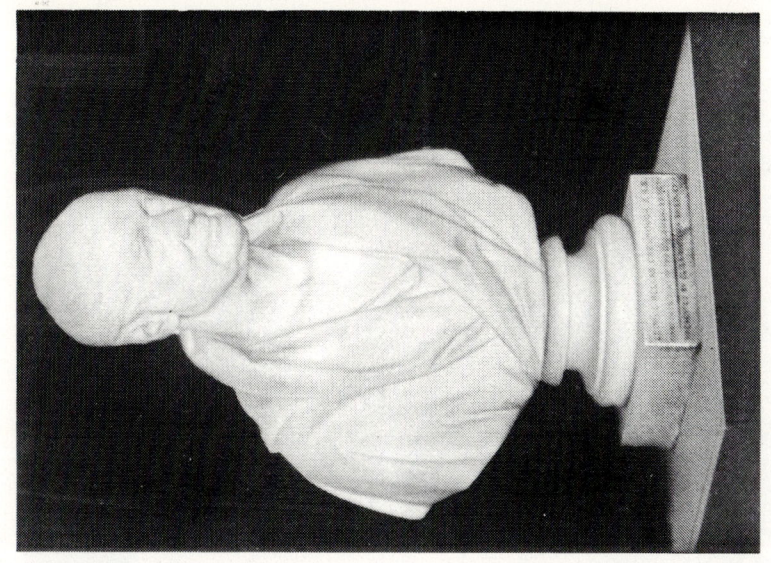

53 G. B. Greenough, F.R.S., founder of the Geological Society (in Geological Museum, London) : 1850.

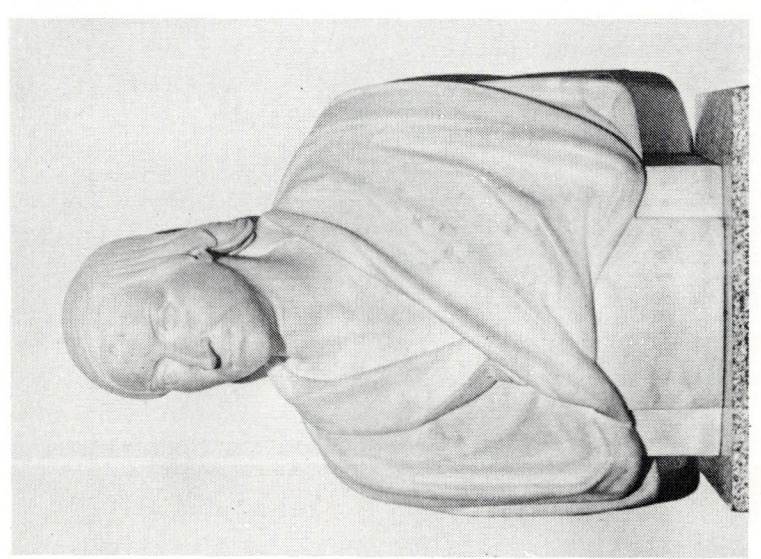

52 Professor Edward Forbes : marble by Burnard (in Geological Museum, London).

54 Marble bust of William Makepeace Thackeray, the novelist, posthumoulsy
executed (about 1867). Copy now at National Portrait Gallery.

55   Medallion of Olive Louise Burnard,
aged 2 ; executed by Burnard in 1875.

SACRED TO THE MEMORY OF
MICHAEL WILLIAMS, ESQRE, M.P.,
OF SCORRIER HOUSE AND CAERHAYS CASTLE, IN THIS COUNTY,
AND OF GNATON HALL, IN DEVONSHIRE.
HE DIED AT TREVINCE, IN THIS PARISH, ON THE 15TH OF JUNE 1858,
AGED 74 YEARS.

56   Memorial to Michael Williams, engineer (in Gwennap Church) ;
reputedly by Burnard.

57   Harry Dawe.   58   Frederick Dawe.

59   Miss (? Bessy) Dawe.   60   Lizzie Jope, neé Dawe.

61 Maud Dawe.

62 Gertie Dawe.

Not Dead but Sleeping

As, calm and beautiful in death she lay,
We gazed on her that from our hearts was reft
And saw the Robber, faltering in his theft
Had stolen the fire but not the charms away,
For, that was there the Spoiler could not slay,
That dared the venom of his deadliest shaft
That branch of Life heaven's Gardner doth engraff
On earth's frail plants that wither in a day

Still, on that face our inmost souls adored
Reposed a child-like, half-celestial smile
As if to heaven or earth, in little while
She might be wafted, or again restored
As if, in crossing Death's mysterious ford
She midway rested on some happy isle.

Nevill N Burnard

63-64 Poems inscribed in the Dawes' Album.

Sonnet.

On Lottie's Birthday. May 29 - 1870.

This is her birthday - O! that I might bring
As a sweet offering to our darling's Tomb,
A garland, cull'd from all the flowers that bloom
Throughout the fairest provinces of Spring:
If to celestials earthly memories cling,
Our thoughts of what she loved while here she
Till her dear form was neath the violets (stayed
                                         laid
Might tempt her hitherward her way to wing.
An Angel whispers,
            "All the world of flowers,
"Father! is now unfolded to my sight,
"Death did but fill the cup of my delight,
And woke to endless life my latent powers,
Still am I yours - and will unseen, requite
Your love with wreaths from amaranthine
                              (bowers.

                Neville K Barnard

* She was particularly fond of flowers.

63-64 Poems inscribed in the Dawes' Album.

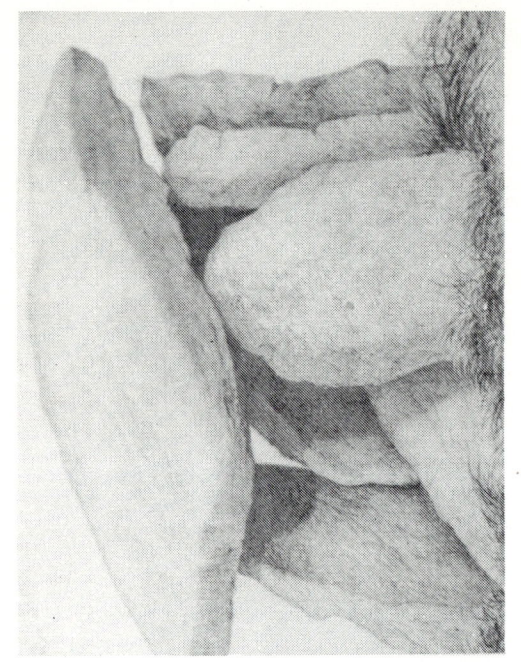

66 Trethevy Quoit (drawn for the Dawes' Album).

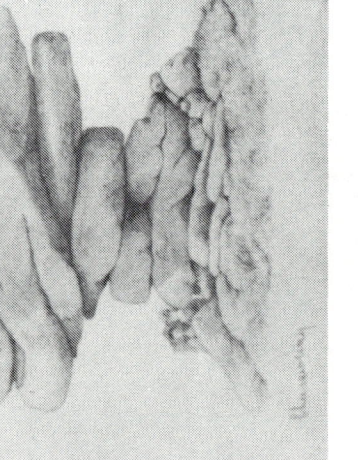

65 Burnard's pencil drawing of the
    Cheesewring.

68 The face Burnard could not caricature (from the Dawes' Album).

67 Pencil portrait of Samuel Drew, metaphysician, by Burnard (from Dawes' Album).

69   Rev. Hugh Rogers : one of Burnard's finest marble sculptures
(in Camborne Church).

70   Slate tombstone erected in memory
of Burnard by Camborne Old Cornwall
Society.

to suggest that Mr. Leaden might assist my views by giving a notice of my bust of Elliott in his paper. I did not see that it would be of any immediate advantage to me at the time, and, I do not see the good of taxing people's good nature when there is no occasion for it, but now I think the time has arrived when a notice of the model may be of service to me, and I therefore shall gladly accept of the assistance which through your influence, I shall easily be able to obtain.

I will not ask you for "your vote and interest" in this monument affair, as I know that you will act in the matter in such a manner as you think will be most conducive to honouring the memory of your departed friend, and under such circumstances, it would be presumptuous in me, to expect that any consideration would make you turn aside from that course. You will easily appreciate my feelings in this matter, I am a great admirer of Elliott and one of "the people" who ought to be grateful to him. I am also ambitious that my name may be associated with such a *lustrous* name as his, and I am sure you cannot blame me for this. I should not make such executions as I have made from mere mercenary motives, I would wish to give full "value received' for every farthing of the money subscribed, as my proposition to the committee and subscribers will shew, and I only wish to have this lasting opportunity of showing that my love for "the poet of the poor" has somewhat of reality in it.

I am Dear Sir
Yours truly,
Neville Burnard.

From the West Briton, 30th January, 1852.

(Extract from Commemorative Poem on Ebenezer Elliott, by Neville N. Burnard.)

Toilers ! Who now have sought the hallowed shrine,
Where Elliott stood, where still his spirit dwells ;
Listen ! And ye will hear his voice divine,
Speak in the music of the mounts and dells ;
Unto your hearts are those sweet sounds addressed,
They call you from the murky town away,
To see a charm on all the landscape rest,
To hear the joyous birds on every spray,
To feel the untainted breeze around you gently play.

.   .   .   .   .

Yet, though his gentle spirit lingers still
By Rivelin and Rother, — unto me

49

Oft comes his voice from Win's majestic hill,
Like the low thunder of a distant sea. —
Now can he mingle with the whirling storm ;
On the fierce arrows of the lightning ride, —
Float on the breeze, exalting, that the worm
Which vexed his struggling soul, hath pined and died ;
Leaving him evermore, a bard beatified.

His soul that battled with ignoble days,
Hath launched on an eternity of bliss ;
And if aught earthly *now* can in him raise
A higher ecstacy, it will be *this* ;
To see ye ponder well the truths he taught,
In the same haunts where he enraptured trod ;
Keeping the field where he so nobly fought,
Resisting Vice and fell Oppression's rod,
Faithful unto yourselves, your country, and your God.

The poor have lost a champion and a guide,
One who could teach them to be truly free ;
Yet though their chief hath fallen, sweet bard of Hyde,*
May they not look with hopeful eyes to thee ?
For thou canst sing in sweetly pleasing strains,
Of all the charms that should their souls inspire ;
And, of their wrongs, adversities, and pains,
Like Elliott, thou canst speak in words of fire !
On thee his mantle falls, to thee he leaves his lyre !

* J. C. Prince, whose poem on Elliott precedes Burnard's in the
news paper column.

Letter from Burnard to his daughter, Sarah Jane.

11 Hugh Street,
Pimlico, S.W.
August 24th, 1873.

Dear Jennie,
    Just a few words to say we are all pretty well or " just as usual."
We have come through the thunder-storm safe and sound. Yesterday
about 5 p.m. the sky was almost suddenly darkened. I never saw
anything like it before. Then it came on to rain and lighten and
thunder as though it meant it and the lightning continued until
past midnight. As I was going along the Wilton Road on Saturday
night I met Binden the Painters, who told me he was at work at
Crabbett and he offered to take anything that we might want to
send you. He called last evening just as the storm was clearing a
little to know if we wanted to send anything but Mamma was so

upset by the thunder that she could not think of anything that you might want. I sent three modelling tools and a pair of compasses by him to Mr. Penfold that belonged to Mr. Blunt that I had brought home in mistake among my tools.

We all hope you will be very careful and not eat too many green apples. I know that children are liable to do such things when they have a chance and that is why I caution you. If I thought you would take it I would send you a " prophy " or two. The above mixing of the singular and the plural is bad grammer but the meaning is all right. I have nothing to tell you in the way of news, that is, nothing smaller than a thunder storm which I have told you of already.

We are all just as usual and that you know already also, so no more at present from

Your affectionate Father

(instead of a signature here
follows a small drawing of himself:
face and curly head.)

Extract from verses sent by Neville Burnard to Charles F. Burnard of Mannamead, Plymouth

My lately found, but firm and trusty friend,
Whose sires with mine their Cornish blood *might* blend,
Or might *not*, still, I prize you all the same,
Though Goldsmith says " What's friendship but a name ? "
The adage tells us, though, " A friend in need "
Is, turn it as you may, " A friend indeed."

I could not let this genial happy day
Without one word of greeting pass away,
Without a wish, most heartily express'd ;
That you and yours may evermore be bless'd —
Here, with the best that Fortune's hands can give —
There, with our fathers, " gone before," to live.

'Tis not for me to point you name by name,
Nor tell why *either* more regard should claim
Than all the rest — still, there's *one* little love
In whom are met the Olive branch and Dove,
Whose tender face hath grown a " charm " to me,
Which, in the dark, *I shut my eyes and see* !
And ask in such a temple, whether sin
Could, in so pure a soul a votary win ?

Her merry dimples, her sweet laughing eyes,
Where every charm with yet another vies,
Until, with wonderment, *our* eyes run o'er
At some new beauty, never seen before . . .

The above refers to Olive Louise Burnard, sculpted by N.N.B. (see illustration 55). Lady Sayer, the daughter of Olive Louise, writes :

I enclose photographs of the little portrait medallion or plaque of my mother aged 2 by Neville Northy Burnard and also of the small statuette/bust of Richard Lander attributed to N.N.B. As you may know, N.N.B. never saw Lander, but worked from the Royal Geographical Society's portrait of him. Lander's daughter was very like him, and sat to N.N.B. " in the presence of Brockedon's picture, to assist him in modelling the face." I think the little statuette may have been a trial piece. It has always been reputed to be by Neville Burnard.

My mother's portrait is indisputably by him. I have a letter written to her in 1967 by one of her cousins, Florence (Floss) Headly, who was aged 6 at the time N.N.B. modelled it in 1875 at my grand-father's or great-grandfather's house in Plymouth ; N.N.B. could have been staying with either. The letter says ". . . I can remember N.N.B. quite well, when he was doing that one of you. I must have been somewhere about 6 or 7. I can see him now, sitting with his back to the fire, at the end of the dining room table. I disliked him intensely, as whenever I went near him he threatened to dab me with clay, and I think he must have done so, as I disliked him so much ! "

He was, however, enchanted by my mother (Olive Burnard) and sent the (foregoing) poem to my great-grandfather Charles F. Burnard after one of his visits to him, with the request that it be read at Christmas dinner when the pudding was brought in.

Line written by Burnard on the death of an eleven year old boy at Altarnun : 1877.

Let them not weep ; the time draws daily nearer,
When they will end this more protracted race
When each to each shall closer be and dearer
Than in their subluminary dwelling place.
Then all will be revealed that now is hidden,
All doubts will pass away, all slanders flee,
At that celestial feast where all are bidden—
So tell my parents not to mourn for me !

None in the Wilderness would wish to wander
Whose feet hath trodden once the Promised Land.
Believe that all is well, nor pause to ponder
On things that mortals cannot understand.
He is most blessed that is the firmest trusting,
Believing One that wiser far than he
Is for his good that balance still adjusting ;
So tell my parents not to mourn for me !

I now can see what might have been my story
Had I remained through man's allotted days :
Sorrow for joy, dark age for youth and glory ;
O bless the love that hastened me away
And wafted me across that mystic river
Where all discordant elements agree,
Calmed by His word that can from Death deliver.
So tell my loved one not to weep for me !

Mss. in possession of Mr. F. J. Herring.

Letter from Thomas Burnard to John Sandercock, Esq.

> 75 Sutherland Street,
> Gloucester Street,
> Pimlico,
> London S.W.
> May 6th, 1889.

Dear Sir,

I wrote to Richard Kittow, Esq. on the 29th of April last and received a reply upon the 1st inst. referring me to you as able to give me all the information I require.

In 1885 and 1886 an Arbitration was held to decide the common right and the ownership of Trewint Marsh and Wint Down. Jonathan Nicholls, Esq. was declared *high lord*.

Now the *property* belonged to my great great grandfather Nicholas Burnard of St. Breward & Altarnun and was willed away to his 2 sons, Wife & six daughters. The Wife obtained probate in 1779 upon this will and estates.

But though it descends in a direct unbroken line to me, *I was never consulted,* neither was my existence acknowledged but ignored.

I have a copy of this bogus Arbitration.

What I should feel obliged to you for is if you can give me the names of the Tenants now in Trewint, the whole of which I claim, and the length of tenure Mr. Jasper has occupied Trefolls and who he bought of.

If you can tell me the extent of the Pentpond Estate originally in possession of George Burnard, son of Nicholas, I should be extremely obliged.

You will excuse the audacity of a stranger I hope when I tell that my Father Neville Northy Burnard was a pupil of Mr. Sandercock of North Hill and further that Henery (*sic*) Sandercock his son was a great friend both of my own and father's. Mr. Kittow also was a great friend of Father's.

I am yours most
respectfully
Thomas Burnard.

APPENDIX B

A DEFENCE OF THE MINISTRY OF THE CHURCH OF ENGLAND

This drawing by Neville N. Burnard at the early age of 13 is charged with peculiar interest. Though the original book with its title-page is unknown, as regards date of publication, contents of volume and author, the incipient skill and meticulous exactitude of Burnard's 'Copy' is quite extraordinary, and well portrays the rich promise of his more mature works, mostly in the realm of Sculpture. Central in the Drawing is the concept of Scripture as the Pillar and ground of truth with text from I. Timothy 3 : 15 written in *Greek*; but superimposed upon the Pillar is the Heraldic scroll containing "A Defence of the Ministry and Ministers of the Church of England" by Rev. John Auden D.D., written in *English*, while the base of the Pillar appears to contain the names of the various Ministers associated with Dr. Auden, but the names etc. are all in Latin. Flanked on the Left is a Figure - Armed Prudence (symbolical of Law and Order) while on the Right is a typical Clerical Figure, representing Learned Piety. The surrounding embellished scroll work contains various Proof-Texts all in English, with sundry Angelic figures, and a shining Sun.

At the bottom of the Drawing, and behind the Armed Prudence figure sits a Lion, symbolising Power, while just behind the Ministerial Figure appears a Lamb symbolising Innocence or Meekness.

The Message of the Drawing suggests in Artistic pictorial imagery, that Ministers of our Lord are called to implement their sacred vows, by contending for the supremacy of the Scriptures of Truth in all humility and Evangelical grace; while similarly, the Custodians of Justice, armed with the panoply of Power and impressive regalia of High Office, are expected to support and sustain the Gospel Message, under the scorching light of the Sun of Righteousness and the Heavenly scrutiny of Angelic Beings.

APPENDIX C

Extract from article by Lawrence Maker in the Western Morning News of 23rd March, 1954:

Mary Ann Burnard left her London home at 11 Hugh Street, and hurried to Portland to nurse her brother, Tom Nicholson. She took her two youngest children with her, and both contracted scarlet fever. Lottie, the younger, only 11 years old, died on March 7, 1870, and Tom died the day after. They were buried together in the churchyard at St. Nicholas, Broadwey, near Weymouth. To Burnard fell the sad task of carving a headstone for the grave. He chose a unique design. A curtain drawn back revealed a background of stars and against this, facing each other, were the almost life-size profile portraits of man and child, also a broken lily and an artist's palette with brushes—all beautifully carved and bearing the stamp of the master.

APPENDIX D

CHRONOLOGICAL TABLE OF BURNARD'S WORK

Date of Work and Description	Place Where Work Can Be Seen
1830 Shell cameo of James Montgomery	Isbell Cottage, Trewint, Altarnun
1830 Slate tombstone to Grace Burnard	Now in Truro Museum
1831 Hieraspistes : A Defence of the Ministry of the Church of England.	Drawing in the possession of Mrs. Grace Kittow, Bude).
1831 Slate head of Homer.	Library at the Polytechnic Society, Falmouth
1832 Slate tombstone to Burnard's grand-parents	Altarnun churchyard
1833 Tombstone to William and Ann Webb	Bodmin Church
1833 Tombstone to Arthur Peter.	North Hill churchyard
1833 Slate tablet in memory of a local mine agent.	Gwennap Church, north wall
1832-3 Carving and modelling decorations in plaster and stone — possibly by Burnard.	Place House, Fowey
1835 Slate relief of the Laocoön, (1st Silver Medal)	Library at Polytechnic Society, Falmouth
1835? Marble plaque to Elizabeth Willcocks	Fowey church
1836 Carving of Christ bearing the cross (Bronze Medal)	Polytechnic Society, Falmouth
1837 Carving of Jupiter and Thetis (Bronze Medal).	Polytechnic Society, Falmouth
1836 Stone head (in Polyphant) of Wesley	Old Wesleyan Church, Penpont, Altarnun — Also a copy at Truro in the chapel of Lis Escop.

Early years in London. A slate carving of a sow and her family. Various sculptures by Chantrey were partially worked by Burnard. Commissions from Bailey, Marshal, Foley and other leading sculptors.

1841 3 Medallion marble portraits, (1st Silver Medal)	Falmouth Polytechnic Society Exhibition
1843 Contentment — an unfinished group (Silver Medal)	Falmouth Polytechnic Society Exhibition
1847 Marble bust of Dr. Carlyon	Truro Council Chamber.
1847 Marble bust of Prince of Wales	Exhibited first at the Poly. exh., the R.A. in 1848 ; at the Great Exhibition 1851. Now at Falmouth Polytechnic Society
1848 Bust of a child	Exhibited at the R. Academy.
1849 Bronze casting bust of John Couch Adams	Exhibited at the Royal Academy Now at Royal Astronomical Society In Launceston Museum
1849 Bust of Sir Charles Lemon	Exhibited at Royal Academy
1850 Bust of G. B. Greenhough, F.R.S. (founder of Geol. Soc. 1778-1855)	Presented in 1859 to Geological Museum by Miss E. M. Smedley, (now in the library there)
1850 Bust of General Lord Gough	
1851 Medallion portrait of 84 year-old fish-wife Mary Kelynack	Exhibited at Polytechnic Society Exhibition, Falmouth
1851 Bust of C. W. Peach — (coast-guard — naturalist. F.R.P.S.E.)	Exhibited at Poly. Soc. Exh., also in 1852 exhibited at R.A.
1851 The Prince of Peace (bust)	Exhibited at the Great Exhibition

1851	Bust of Beethoven, prepared for Frederick Beale, Treasurer of the Musical Union — of Cranmer & Beales Music shop, Regent Street	Exhibited in 1851 & 1852 at R.A.; received 1st Silver Medal at Polytechnic Society, Falmouth
1852	Bust of Kossuth	Exhibited at Polytechnic Society, Falmouth
1852	Statue of Richard Lander	Lemon Street, Truro
1853	Bust of Harriet Beecher Stowe	Intended for Crystal Palace, presented to committee of British and Foreign Anti-Slavery Soc. by the Anti-Slavery Cause
1854	Statue of Ebenezer Elliot	Set up in Market Square — Sheffield, 1875 : removed to Weston Park
1854	Rev Robert Newton	Wesley Chapel, City Road, London
1855	Bust of Prof. Edward Forbes, F.R.S. (Silver Medal)	1867. Exhibited at R.A. Original is in Isle of Man — a copy by I.C. Lough is in the Geological Museum, London.
1855	Small medallion (Father Gavazzi) Self-portrait medallion	Sent to Polytechnic Society, Falmouth
1855	Bust of Gerald Massey (poet and mystic)	Sent to Polytechnic Society Falmouth
1858	The Corn-Law Rhymer	Exhibited at Royal Academy
1858	Bust of James Montgomery	Exhibited at Royal Academy
1858?	Marble bust and tablet to the Reverend Hugh Rogers	Exhibited at Royal Academy Camborne Parish Church
1866	The late Richard Cobden	Exhibited at Royal Academy
1866	Marble bust of Erwin Harvey Wadge of Lewannick - mining expert	Bought for £105 by West-country miners
1867?	Bust of W. M. Thackeray (posthumous). Copy in National Portrait Gallery, London	Exhibited at Royal Academy. Intended for the Cottonian Library, Plymouth. Now lost, presumably blitzed.
1868?	Bust and tablet to Dr. George Smith	Wesley Chapel, Camborne
1869	The Rt. Hon. John Bright, M.P. (marble)	Exhibited at Royal Academy
1870	Memorial to Lottie Burnard and Tom Nicholson	In churchyard of St. Nicholas, Broadwey, Weymouth
1871	The Rt. Hon. C. P. Villiers, M.P.	Exhibited at Royal Academy
1871	The Rt. Hon. W. E. Gladstone, M.P. John Benjamin Smith.	Exhibited at Royal Academy
?	(Lady Durning Lawrence's father)	Exhibited at Royal Academy
1873	E. A. Leatham, Esq., M.P.	Exhibited at Royal Academy
1876	Pencil portrait of Betty Venning (née Burnard), aged 82, of St. Clether	In possession of Mr. J. Venning
1875	Medallion of Olive Louise Burnard	In possession of Lady Sayer
1875-6	Pencil portraits of members of the Dawe family, of Crow's Nest, St. Cleer, and sketches of the Cheesewring and Trethevy Quoit ; in bound album	In possession of Mr. Trewin Copplestone, Bourton, Berks.

VERSE BY BURNARD :
Poems in West Briton : 1849, Lines Written on the Celebration of the Birth of Burns ; Jan. 30th, 1852, The Corn Law Rhymer (seven stanzas on the Death of Ebenezer Elliott).
Poems and satires in the Dawes' Album (see above).

APPENDIX E

MISCELLANEOUS WORKS — UNDATED

Tombstone to Robert Nicholl in Altarnun Churchyard.

3 shields carved for the National Schools at Tywardreath, Cornwall.

Slate carving, The Schoolmistress ; acquired by F. R. Rodd of Trebartha Hall (lost).

Medallion in plaster of Mr. J. S. Enys.

Self-portrait medallion in plaster, now in Truro Museum.

Medallions in plaster of Burnard's mother ; in Truro Museum.

Medallions of other members of his family (lost ?).

Slate medallion of a caricatured profile (early work) ; in Truro Museum.

Marble bust of Richard Trevithick, in Truro Museum.

Marble medallion of Mrs. Catherine Enys (daughter of Davies Gilbert) — in Truro Museum.

Pencil drawing of Rev. William Rowe, Vicar of St. Teath ; in Truro Museum.

Plaster bust of Dr. William Borlase, in Truro Museum.

Pencil drawing of an unknown gentleman, in Truro Museum.

Medallion of Mrs. Elizabeth Heard (in Truro, a private home).

Life size medallion of Mr. Benallack (a lawyer) ; whereabouts unknown.

Marble bust of Admiral Boscawen (executed from plaster model by Roubiliac, for the Earl of Falmouth).

Bust of Joseph Thomas Treffry in Place House, Fowey.

Busts of Hon. Mrs. Tremayne, Charles Dickens, and Charles Buller : whereabouts all unknown.

The hand of Richard Cobden, sculpted in white marble ; commissioned for the Fine Art Galleries, Brighton, by John Bright.

Bust of Michael Williams, engineer, of Scorrier.

Memorial to Michael Williams, engineer, in Gwennap Church.

Bust of Richard Lander (believed by Burnard) in the possession of Lady Sayer.

Pencil portrait of Emily Herring, in possession of Mr. W. Honey, Bodmin.

Pencil drawing of John Vosper of Tredawle, Altarnun, in possession of Mr. F. J. Herring of Bissoe.

Pencil drawing of Emma Bath of Trenilk, Five Lanes, in possession of Mr. F. J. Herring.

Pencil portrait of Edward Nicholls Vosper, of Altarnun, in possession of Mrs. R. Grenfell, Barnstaple.

Bust of William Bickford Smith, M.P., of Trevarno, in Trevarno House, Helston.

Pencil portraits of Henry Richards and Jane Richards, of Crowntown, in possession of Mr. R. L. Nicholas.

Copy of head of John Wesley (as on Meeting House, Altarnun), in chapel of Lis Escop, Truro.

BIBLIOGRAPHY

Berry, Claude. Portrait of Cornwall. Robert Hale, 1963.

Betjeman, John. Cornwall. Shell Guide, 1964.

Bizley, Alice. The Slate Figures of Cornwall. Penzance, 1965.

Davey, F. Hamilton. Neville Northy Burnard. Royal Cornwall Polytechnic Society, Annual Report, Vol I, part 2, 1910.

Davey, F. Hamilton. Penjerrick. The Cornish Magazine, edited by A. T. Quiller-Couch. Vol. 2, 1899.

Fox, Caroline. Memories of Old Friends of Penjerrick, Cornwall from 1835-1871 (Extracts from journals and letters of Caroline Fox). London, 1882.

Gill, Fred C. In the Steps of Wesley. Lutterworth Press, 1962.

Gunnis, Rupert. Dictionary of British Sculptors. Abbey Library.

Baring-Gould, S. Cornish Characters and Strange Events. Bodley Head, 1908.

Jones, George R. A. Sir Francis Chantrey, R.A. London, 1849.

Maker, Lawrence. From Nails to Chisels. Doidge's Annual, 1940.

Maker, Lawrence. A Famous Cornish Sculptor. (In The Post & Weekly News, Launceston, 24.9.68).

Pevsner, N. Buildings of Cornwall. Penguin, 1970.

Polsue, J. Lake's Parochial History of Cornwall. Vol. 1 & Vol. 2. Truro, 1867-73.

Stephen, L. (editor). Dictionary of National Biography Vol. 7, 1886.
Art Union. p. 180 1848.
The Builder, 1852. p. 205.
The Builder, 1854. p. 467.
Museum of Practical Geology : Handbook. 1896.